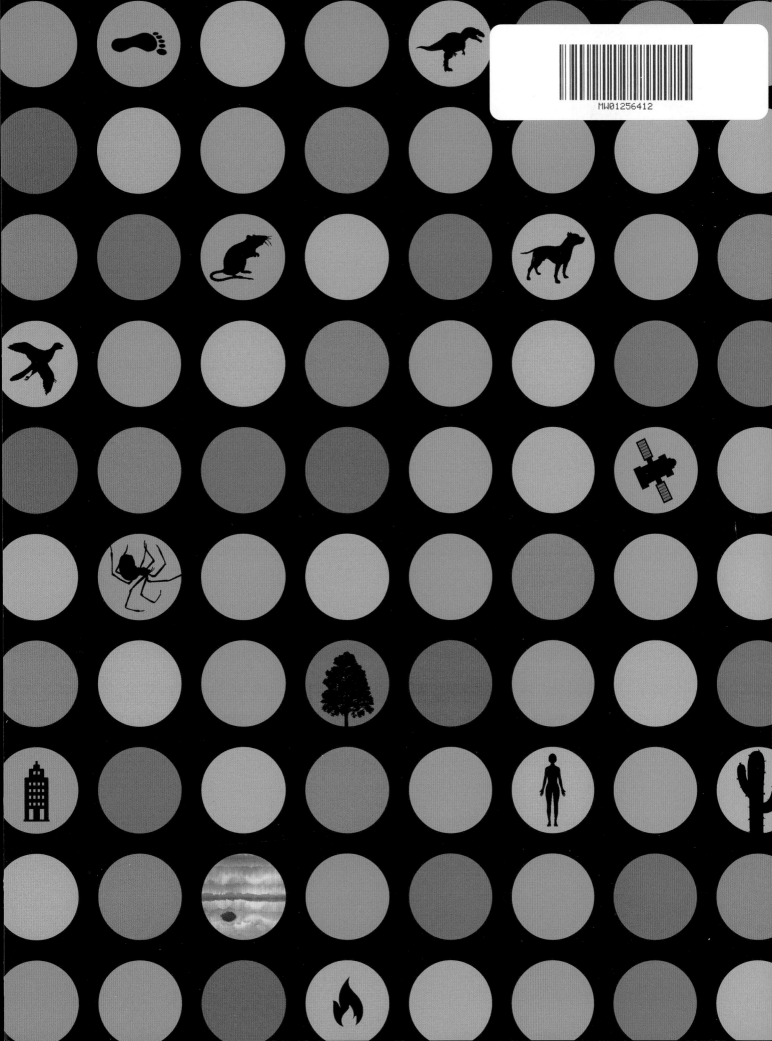

OUR WORLD

BY THE

NUMBERS

STEVE JENKINS

Clarion Books
An Imprint of HarperCollinsPublishers

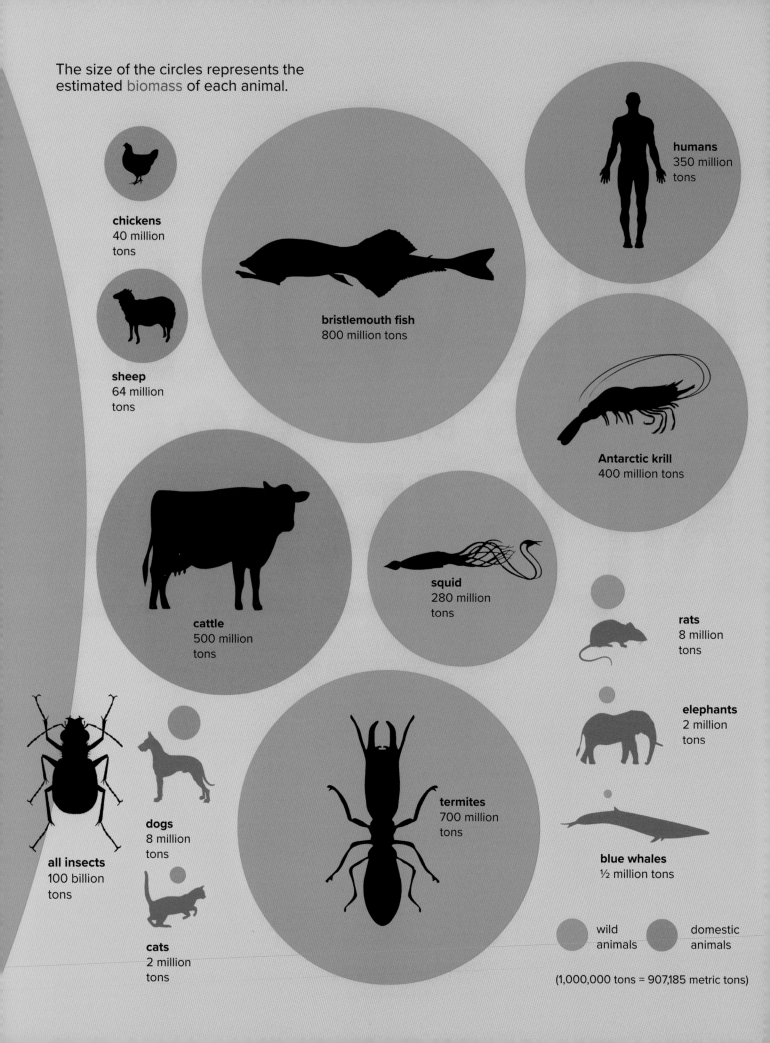

The size of the circles represents the estimated biomass of each animal.

chickens
40 million tons

sheep
64 million tons

bristlemouth fish
800 million tons

humans
350 million tons

Antarctic krill
400 million tons

cattle
500 million tons

squid
280 million tons

rats
8 million tons

elephants
2 million tons

all insects
100 billion tons

dogs
8 million tons

termites
700 million tons

blue whales
½ million tons

cats
2 million tons

wild animals

domestic animals

(1,000,000 tons = 907,185 metric tons)

Numbers help us understand our world. We use numbers to measure and compare things. Numbers help us explain what happened in the past and predict what might happen in the future.

When it comes to understanding our world, numbers are especially important. How old is the Earth? How big is a whale? How high is the tallest mountain? How many people are born every day? It would be difficult to answer these questions—even to ask them—without numbers.

In this book, facts and figures about our world—our place in the solar system, the history of our planet, the people and animals who live here, and all the wondrous things that nature can do—are presented visually as graphs, symbols, and illustrations. These infographics give us another way of looking at the world we live in and understanding some of the amazing things that make it so extraordinary.

Most people have never seen a **bristlemouth**, a small deep-sea fish. But some scientists think that bristlemouths and **termites** might outweigh every other kind of animal. Creatures like these are impossible to count accurately, so estimates of their biomass vary widely.

CONTENTS

The Milky Way Galaxy

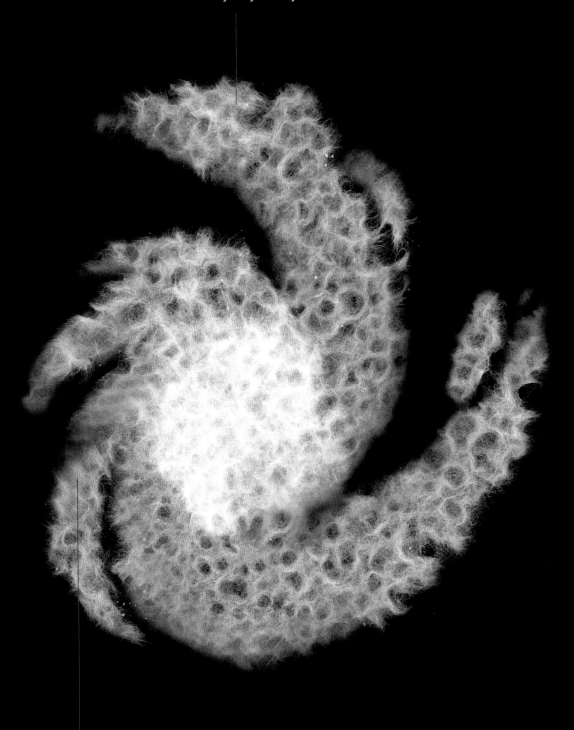

The solar system is here
(but it would be too small to
see in this image).

SOLAR SYSTEM

We live on a small, rocky planet. That planet circles a small, yellow sun. That sun is found near the outer edge of the Milky Way Galaxy. Galaxies are collections of stars—lots of stars. There are hundreds of billions of stars in our galaxy alone. And there are hundreds of billions of other galaxies.

In this chapter, we'll stay closer to home. We'll use infographics to take a closer look at our own Sun and the planets, moons, and other objects that circle it. This is our solar system.

* Words in blue can be found in the glossary on page 154.

What's in our solar system?

Next to some of the giant stars in our galaxy, the Sun is not very big. But compared to everything else in the solar system, it is huge. It contains almost all the matter in the solar system.

Sun

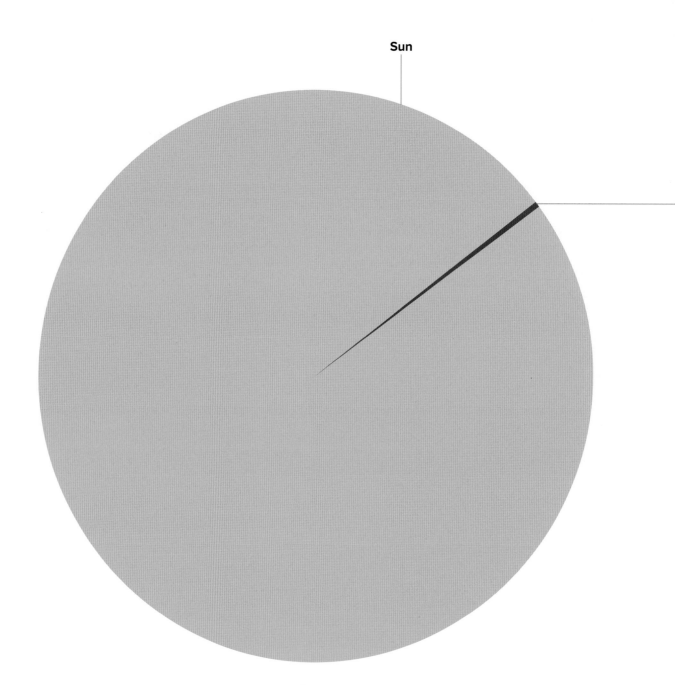

All the matter in the solar system

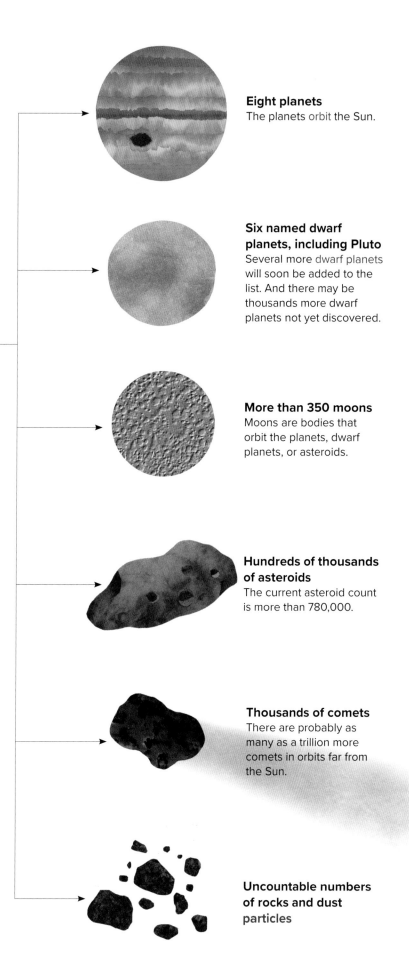

The thin red slice of the circle represents all the matter in the solar system that is *not* part of the Sun.

Eight planets
The planets orbit the Sun.

Six named dwarf planets, including Pluto
Several more dwarf planets will soon be added to the list. And there may be thousands more dwarf planets not yet discovered.

More than 350 moons
Moons are bodies that orbit the planets, dwarf planets, or asteroids.

Hundreds of thousands of asteroids
The current asteroid count is more than 780,000.

Thousands of comets
There are probably as many as a trillion more comets in orbits far from the Sun.

Uncountable numbers of rocks and dust particles

Our star

The word "solar" means "of the Sun."

Temperature at the center of the Sun

27 million°F (15 million°C)

Temperature of the Sun's surface

10,000°F (5,538°C)

Temperature of sunspots (cooler areas on the Sun's surface)

6,400°F (3,500°C)

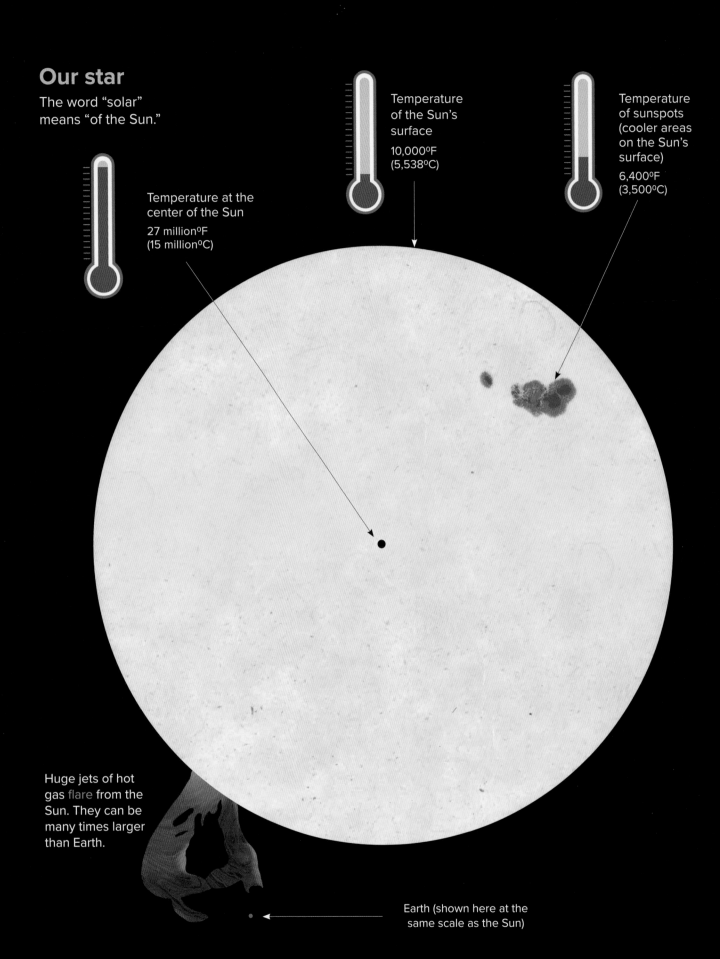

Huge jets of hot gas flare from the Sun. They can be many times larger than Earth.

Earth (shown here at the same scale as the Sun)

A note about temperatures:
F (Fahrenheit) and C (Celsius) are two different temperature scales.

4½ billion years ago

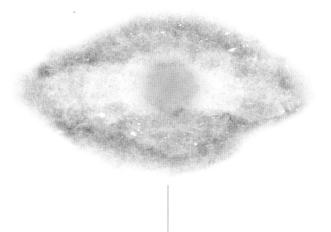

A huge cloud of dust and gas collapses and gets hotter and hotter. The Sun is born.

From about 4 billion years ago to 4 billion years from now

The Sun is a yellow dwarf star, a common type of star in our galaxy.

5 billion years from now

The Sun expands and becomes a red giant star. Earth may be swallowed up by the Sun. But long before that happens, our planet is burned to a crisp.

8 billion years from now

The Sun becomes a white dwarf star, not much larger than Earth but much heavier.

What's an eclipse?

When the Moon passes directly between Earth and the Sun, the Moon casts a shadow on Earth's surface. It's a solar eclipse! When Earth casts its shadow on the Moon, it's called a lunar eclipse.

From Earth, the Sun and Moon appear to be the same size. The Sun is really much larger than the Moon, but it is much farther away.

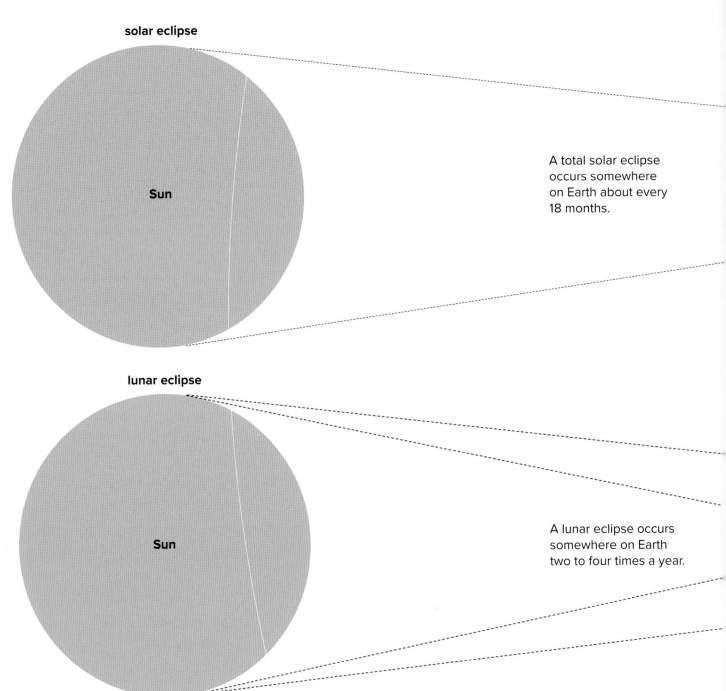

solar eclipse

Sun

A total solar eclipse occurs somewhere on Earth about every 18 months.

lunar eclipse

Sun

A lunar eclipse occurs somewhere on Earth two to four times a year.

Note: Sizes and distances in these diagrams are not to scale.

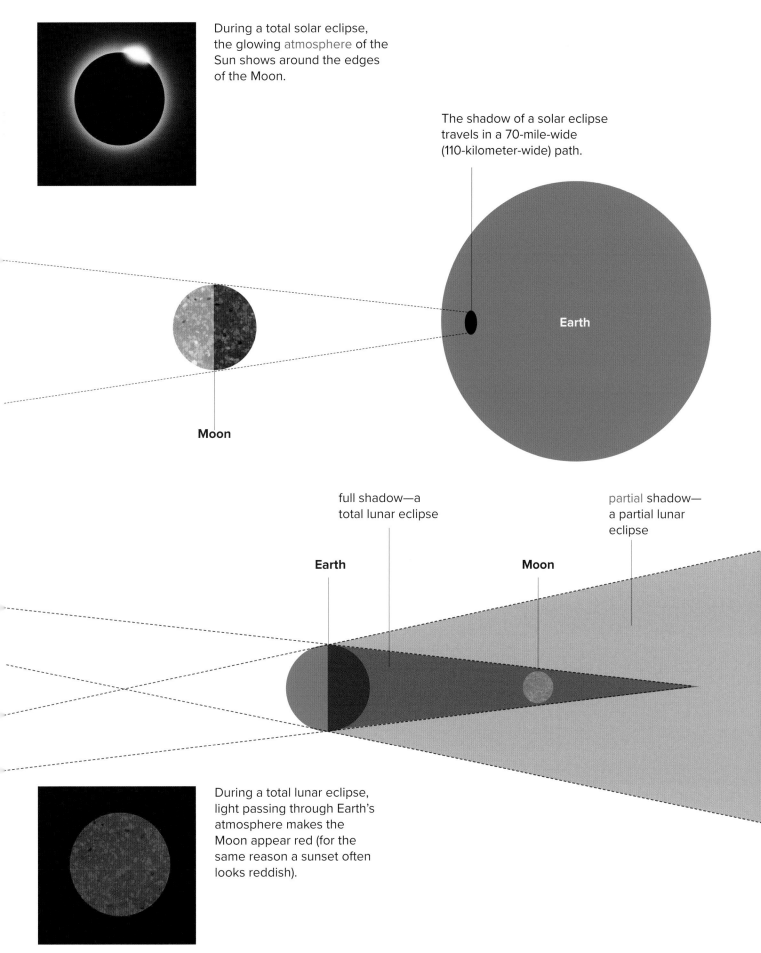

During a total solar eclipse, the glowing atmosphere of the Sun shows around the edges of the Moon.

The shadow of a solar eclipse travels in a 70-mile-wide (110-kilometer-wide) path.

Earth

Moon

full shadow—a total lunar eclipse

partial shadow— a partial lunar eclipse

Earth

Moon

During a total lunar eclipse, light passing through Earth's atmosphere makes the Moon appear red (for the same reason a sunset often looks reddish).

Circling the Sun

All the objects in the solar system— planets, moons, asteroids, and comets—travel in an orbit around the Sun.

This diagram shows the relative distances of the planets from the Sun, but not their actual size. The planets would be too small to see at this scale.

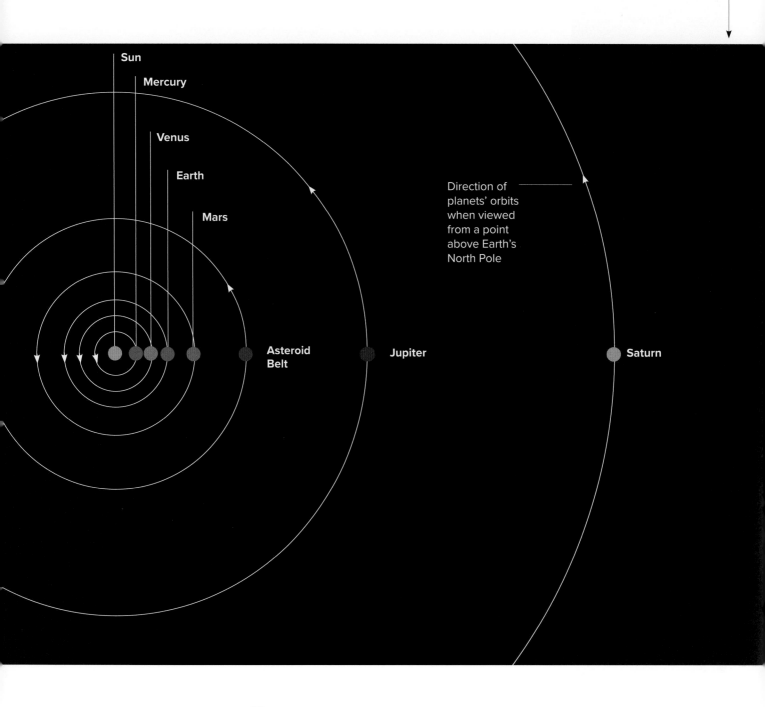

Sun

Mercury

Venus

Earth

Mars

Direction of planets' orbits when viewed from a point above Earth's North Pole

Asteroid Belt

Jupiter

Saturn

1 AU

Measuring the solar system

An **AU**, or **astronomical unit**, is the distance between Earth and the Sun (not shown at actual scale). Astronomers often use AUs to measure distances in the solar system.

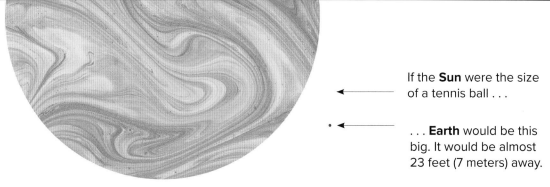

If the **Sun** were the size of a tennis ball . . .

. . . **Earth** would be this big. It would be almost 23 feet (7 meters) away.

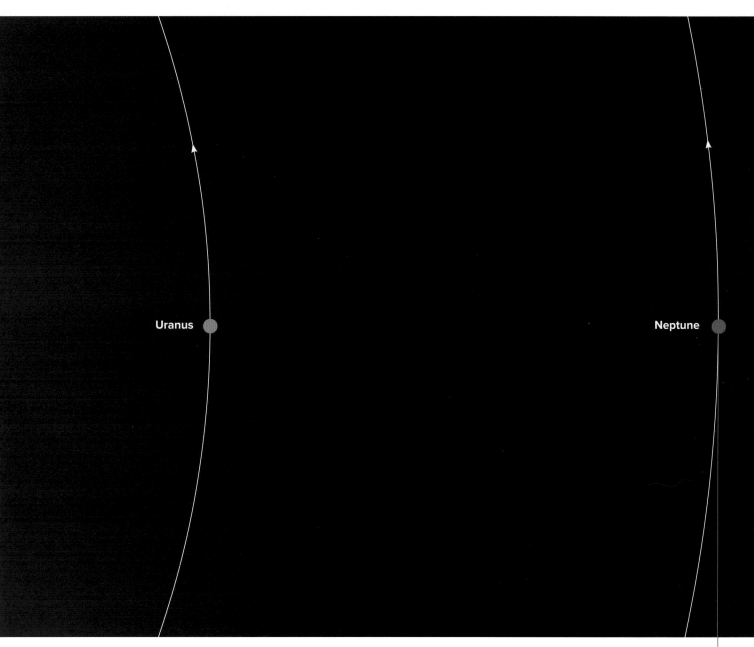

Uranus

Neptune

Neptune is 30 AUs from the Sun.

It is 93 million miles (150 million kilometers) from Earth to the Sun. This is one AU.

How big are the planets?

The inner, or rocky, planets

The gas giants

Venus

Moon

Mars

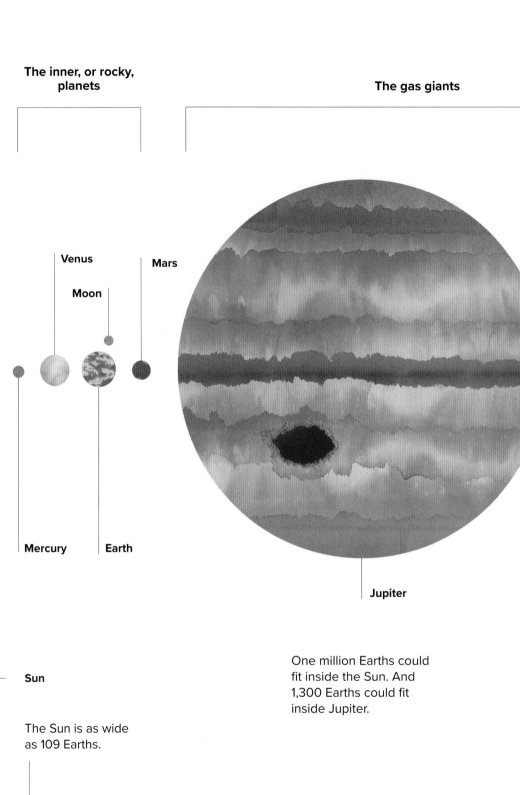

Mercury

Earth

Jupiter

One million Earths could fit inside the Sun. And 1,300 Earths could fit inside Jupiter.

Sun

The Sun is as wide as 109 Earths.

The Sun and the planets are shown here at the same scale.

The ice giants

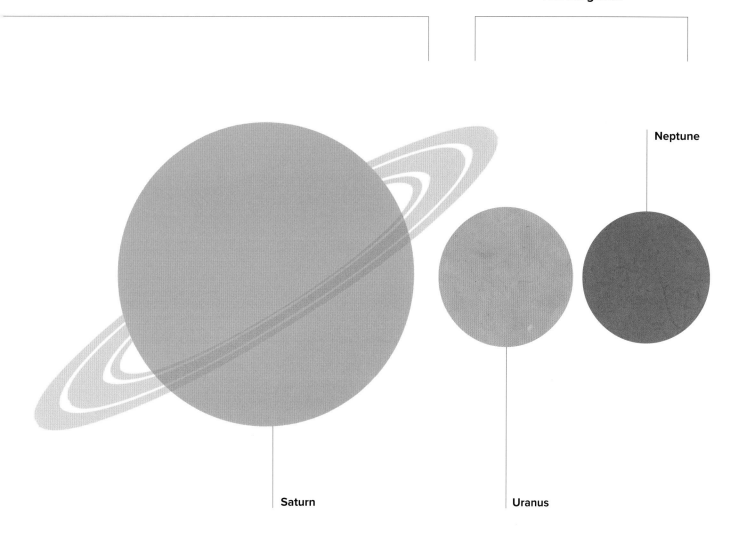

Neptune

Saturn

Uranus

Pluto
(a dwarf planet)

When Pluto was discovered in 1930, it became the solar system's ninth planet. But in 2006, astronomers decided that Pluto is actually a dwarf planet. This left the solar system with just eight planets.

The inner planets

The four planets closest to the Sun are known as the inner, or rocky, planets. They are shown here at the same scale.

Sun

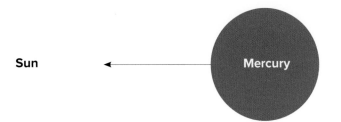

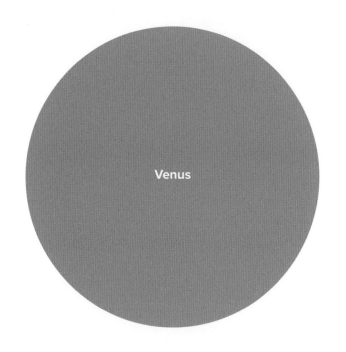

Length of a day
(one full rotation)

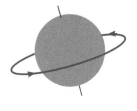

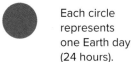
Each circle represents one Earth day (24 hours).

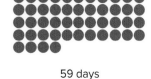
59 days

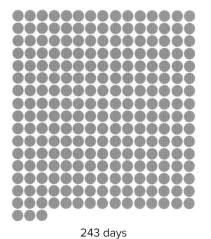
243 days

Length of a year
(one trip around the Sun)

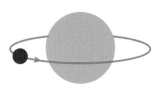

one Earth year (12 months)

88 days

224 days

Number of moons

Mercury

Venus

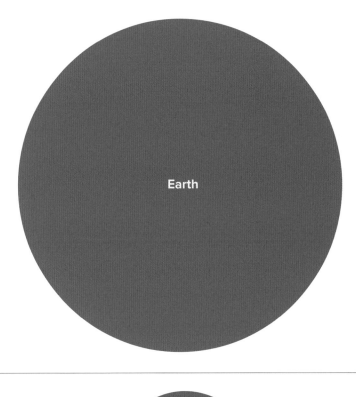

Earth

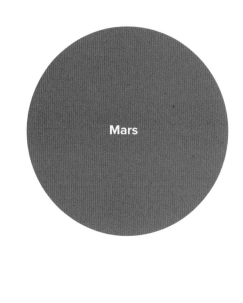

Mars

24 hours

24 hours, 37 minutes

365 days

Earth

687 days

Mars

one moon

two moons

The outer planets

The four outer planets are mostly made of gas and ice.
They are shown here at the same scale.

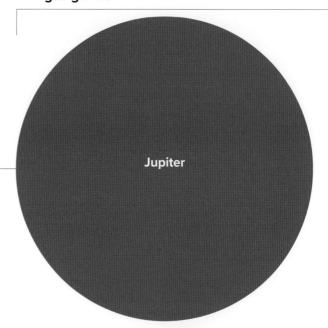

Sun ◄—————————————

Size of Earth
compared to the
outer planets

Jupiter

Length of a day
(one full rotation)

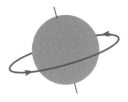

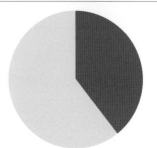

9 hours, 56 minutes

Length of a year
(one trip around
the Sun)

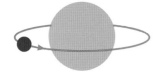

one Earth year
(12 months)

11 years, 11 months

Jupiter

*Note: New moons are
frequently discovered,
so these numbers will
probably change.*

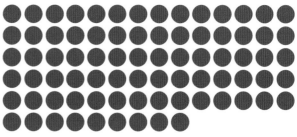

79 moons

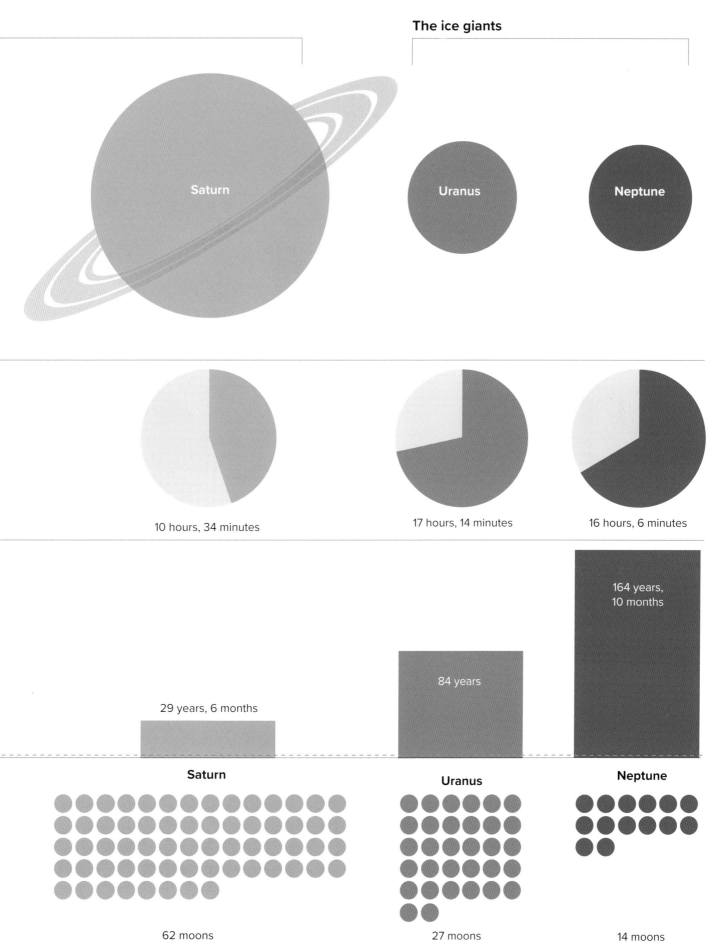

The ice giants

Saturn

Uranus

Neptune

10 hours, 34 minutes

17 hours, 14 minutes

16 hours, 6 minutes

164 years,
10 months

84 years

29 years, 6 months

Saturn

Uranus

Neptune

62 moons

27 moons

14 moons

21

Earth's Moon

Our Moon is the brightest object in the night sky. It's the only place in the solar system—besides Earth—that humans have visited.

The phases of the Moon

The Moon is slowly moving away from Earth. It gets this much farther away each year.

Full Moon

Viewed from Earth, the Moon has phases—it appears to change shape every night.

When the lit-up side of the Moon faces away from us, it's called a New Moon.

Earth and the Moon, showing size and distance at the same scale

Other solar system moons

A moon is a body that orbits a planet, dwarf planet, or asteroid. There are more than 200 moons in our solar system. If a moon is large enough for its own gravity to pull it into a round shape, it is called a *major moon*.

Deimos, a moon of Mars, is small and oddly shaped.

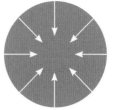

The gravity of a major moon is strong enough to pull it into a sphere.

Major moons of the solar system

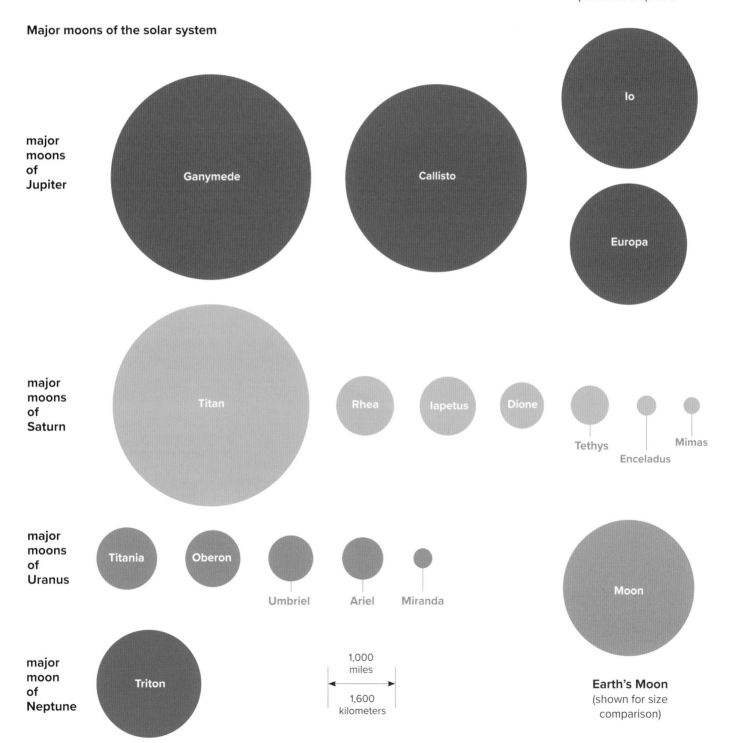

major moons of Jupiter

Ganymede

Callisto

Io

Europa

major moons of Saturn

Titan

Rhea

Iapetus

Dione

Tethys

Enceladus

Mimas

major moons of Uranus

Titania

Oberon

Umbriel

Ariel

Miranda

Moon

major moon of Neptune

Triton

1,000 miles

1,600 kilometers

Earth's Moon
(shown for size comparison)

Asteroids

Between the orbits of Mars and Jupiter are hundreds of millions of asteroids—chunks of rock and ice. They range in size from a few feet across to hundreds of miles in diameter. This part of the solar system is known as the asteroid belt.

Note: This diagram is not to scale.

Mars

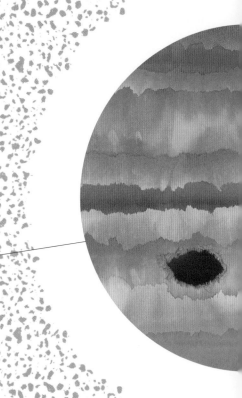

Jupiter

Asteroid Belt

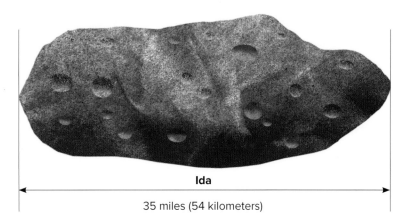

Ida

35 miles (54 kilometers)

Dactyl

This tiny moon is about one mile (1½ kilometers) across.

The asteroid **Ida** looks like a baked potato. And it has a moon of its own, called **Dactyl**. This is the first moon of an asteroid that has been discovered.

Sometimes a piece of an asteroid—or a fragment of a comet—enters Earth's atmosphere. It is called a meteor, or shooting star. If the space rock hits the ground, it is called a meteorite.

Comets

Comets are found in the outer reaches of the solar system, far from the Sun. They are balls of rock, dirt, and ice up to 60 miles (97 kilometers) across.

We have identified a few thousand comets, but there are probably billions or trillions of comets orbiting the Sun.

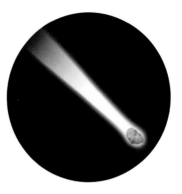

When a comet approaches the Sun, a tail of melted ice and dust streams out behind it. This tail always points away from the Sun.

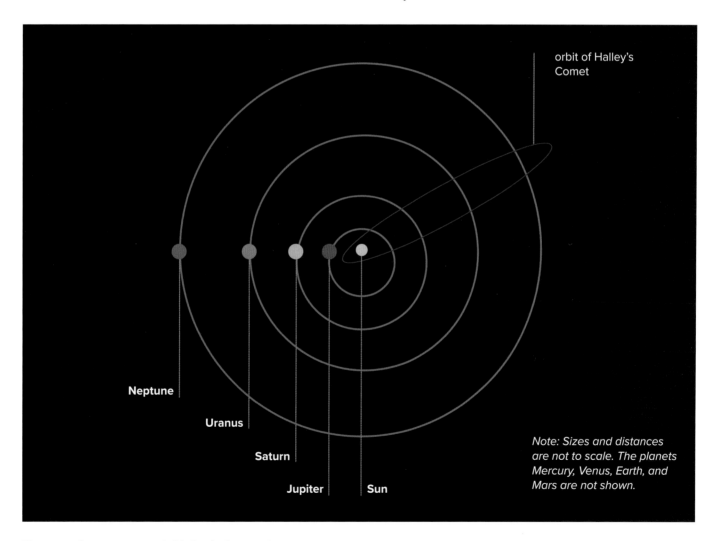

orbit of Halley's Comet

Neptune

Uranus

Saturn

Jupiter

Sun

Note: Sizes and distances are not to scale. The planets Mercury, Venus, Earth, and Mars are not shown.

The most famous comet is **Halley's Comet**. It makes an orbit about every 76 years, and it can easily be seen without a telescope. Halley's Comet will return in 2061.

Many comets make regular orbits of the Sun, some every few years. Other comets take as long as 30 million years to complete one orbit.

Gravity

How high could a person jump on another moon or planet if they can jump three feet high on Earth?

18 feet
(5½ meters)

5 feet
(1½ meters)

4 feet
(122 centimeters)

3 feet
(91 centimeters)

2 feet
(61 centimeters)

1 foot
(30 centimeters)

Gravity is weaker on a small planet. The less gravity there is, the higher a person could jump.

Mercury

Venus

Earth

Moon

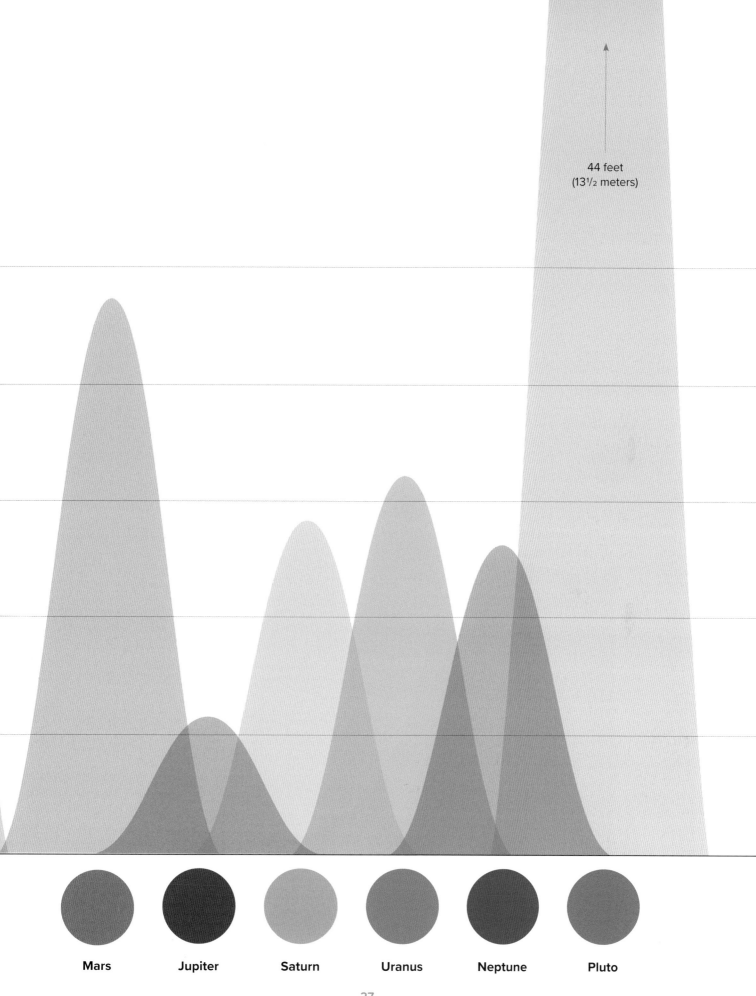

44 feet
(13½ meters)

Mars   **Jupiter**   **Saturn**   **Uranus**   **Neptune**   **Pluto**

Solar system weather

Rain and snow

Earth isn't the only place in the solar system where it rains or snows. But precipitation in other places can be unusual.

 On **Venus** it rains sulfuric acid.

 On **Titan**, a moon of Saturn, it rains methane (liquid natural gas).

 It may rain diamonds on **Jupiter** and other gas giant and ice giant planets.

 Carbon dioxide falls as snow on the poles of **Mars**.

 On **Enceladus**, a moon of Saturn, frozen water falls as snow.

Average temperatures

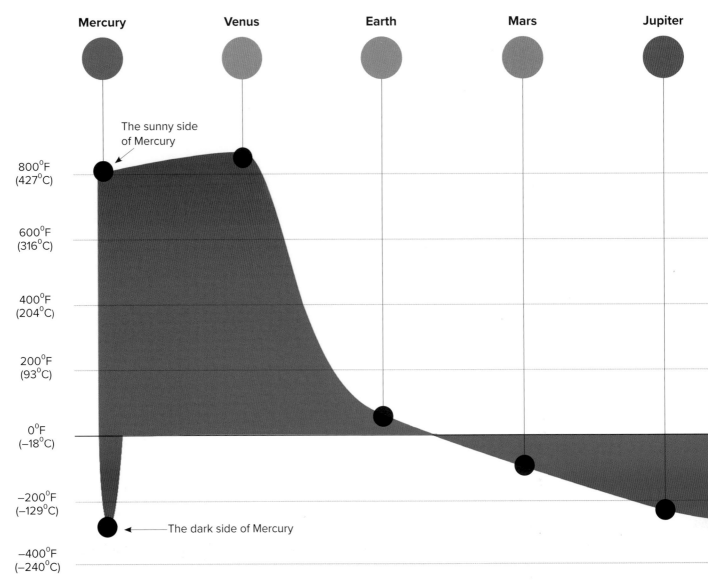

Maximum wind speeds

The solar system can be a windy place.

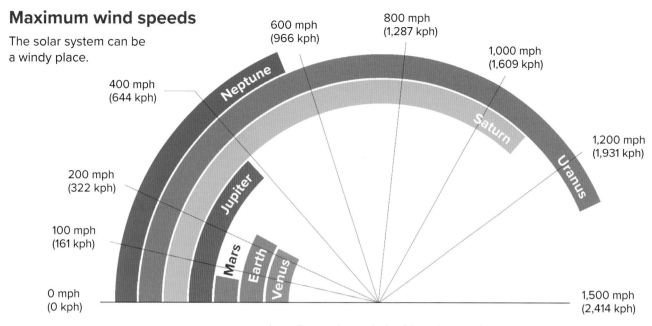

600 mph (966 kph)
800 mph (1,287 kph)
1,000 mph (1,609 kph)
400 mph (644 kph)
1,200 mph (1,931 kph)
200 mph (322 kph)
100 mph (161 kph)
0 mph (0 kph)
1,500 mph (2,414 kph)

Neptune
Jupiter
Mars
Earth
Venus
Saturn
Uranus

mph = miles per hour   kph = kilometers per hour

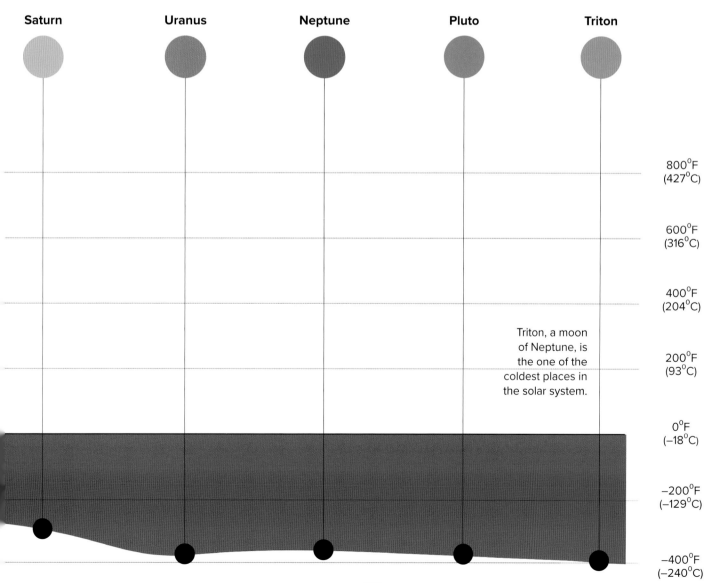

Saturn   Uranus   Neptune   Pluto   Triton

800°F (427°C)

600°F (316°C)

400°F (204°C)

Triton, a moon of Neptune, is the one of the coldest places in the solar system.

200°F (93°C)

0°F (−18°C)

−200°F (−129°C)

−400°F (−240°C)

Solar system discoveries

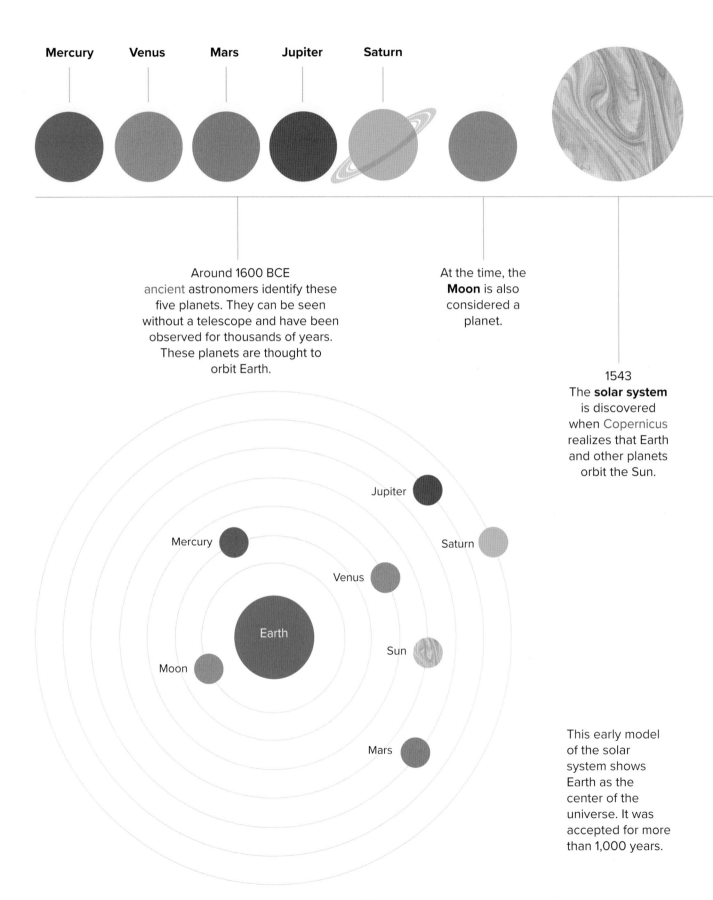

Mercury   **Venus**   **Mars**   **Jupiter**   **Saturn**

Around 1600 BCE ancient astronomers identify these five planets. They can be seen without a telescope and have been observed for thousands of years. These planets are thought to orbit Earth.

At the time, the **Moon** is also considered a planet.

1543
The **solar system** is discovered when Copernicus realizes that Earth and other planets orbit the Sun.

Jupiter

Mercury

Saturn

Venus

Earth

Sun

Moon

Mars

This early model of the solar system shows Earth as the center of the universe. It was accepted for more than 1,000 years.

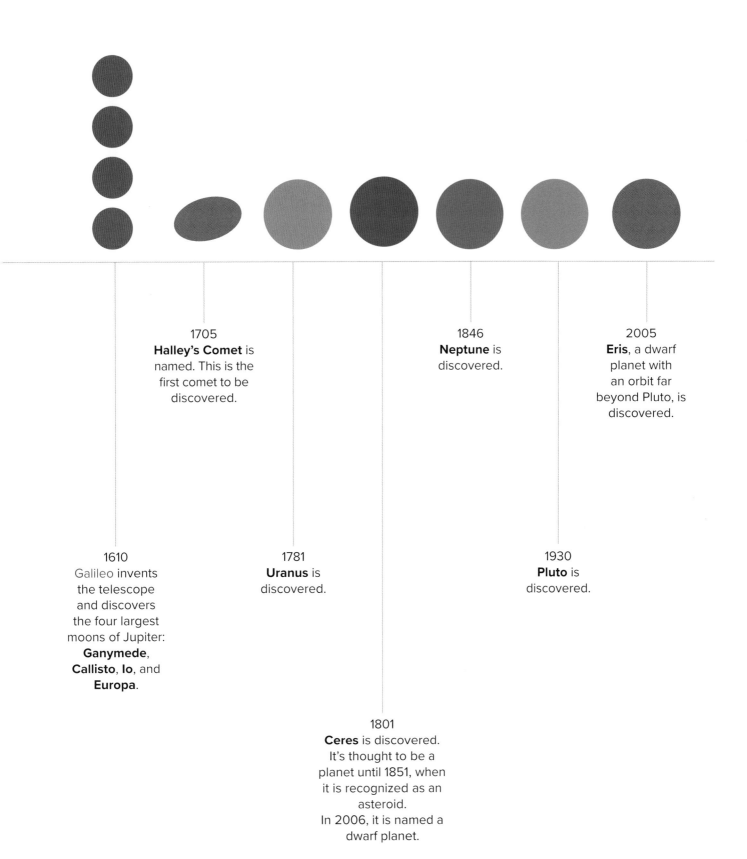

1705
Halley's Comet is named. This is the first comet to be discovered.

1846
Neptune is discovered.

2005
Eris, a dwarf planet with an orbit far beyond Pluto, is discovered.

1610
Galileo invents the telescope and discovers the four largest moons of Jupiter: **Ganymede**, **Callisto**, **Io**, and **Europa**.

1781
Uranus is discovered.

1930
Pluto is discovered.

1801
Ceres is discovered. It's thought to be a planet until 1851, when it is recognized as an asteroid.
In 2006, it is named a dwarf planet.

Exploration

How many times have we visited other places in the solar system?*

Sun		8 satellites
Mercury		4 satellites, 1 rocket
Venus		8 satellites, 7 rockets
Mars		8 satellites, 8 rockets
Asteroids		8 satellites, 4 rockets
Jupiter		9 satellites, 1 rocket
Saturn		4 satellites
Uranus		1 satellite
Neptune		1 satellite
Pluto (dwarf planet)		1 satellite

*As of the end of 2018.

New missions take place frequently, so these numbers will change.

Some of the visits in the chart were made by spacecraft that traveled to more than one planet or moon.

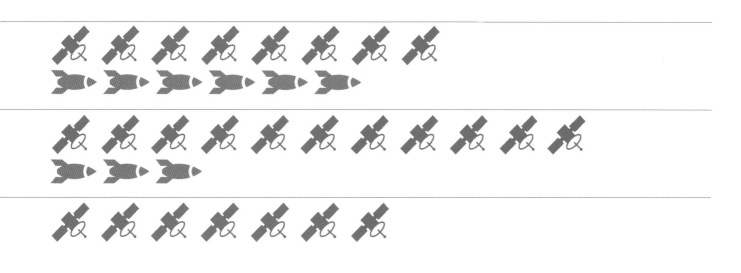

 Orbited or flew by

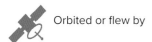 Landed or crashed on the surface

Visits to comets and other planet's moons are not shown.

We have explored Earth's Moon more than any other place in the solar system

 37 orbiters

 30 unmanned landers

 Six human missions have landed on the Moon. Twelve astronauts have walked on its surface.

Animals in space

Humans aren't the only earthlings that have traveled off the planet. From the earliest days of space exploration, animals have been launched into space.

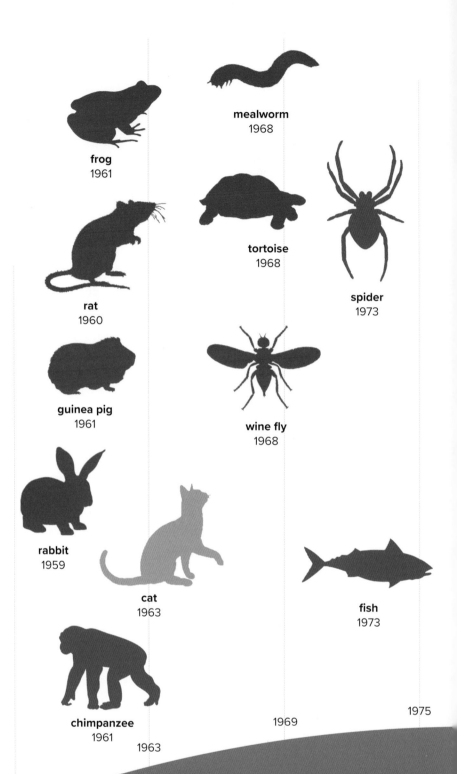

mealworm
1968

frog
1961

tortoise
1968

spider
1973

rat
1960

wine fly
1968

guinea pig
1961

rabbit
1959

cat
1963

fish
1973

chimpanzee
1961

1969

1975

1963

1957

monkey
1949

dog
1951

mouse
1950

fruit fly
1947

1951

1945

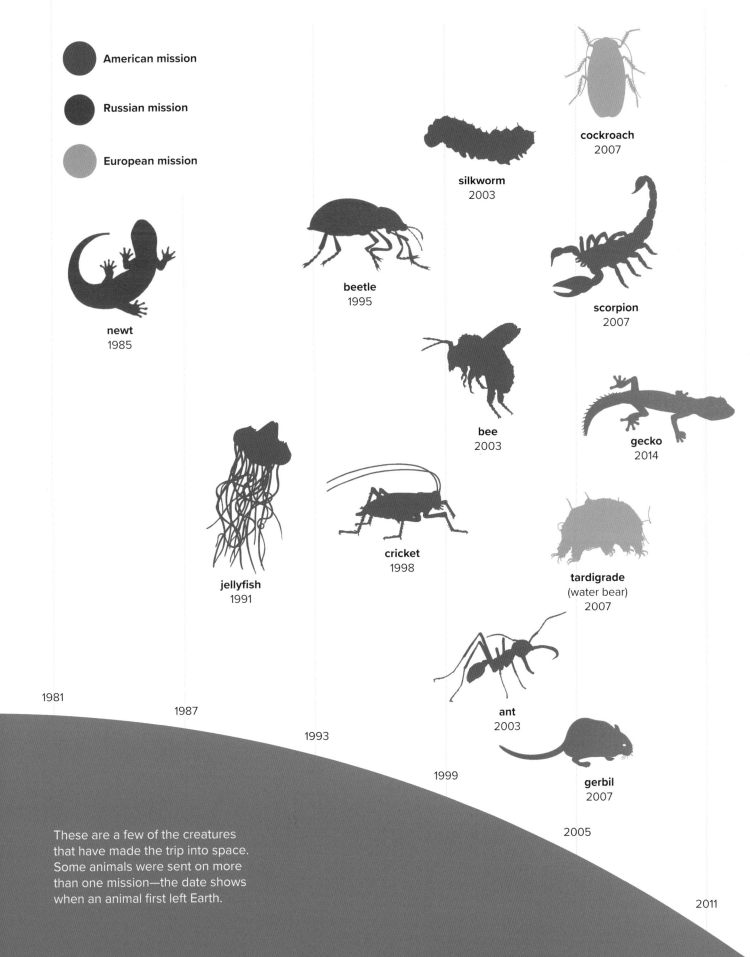

American mission

Russian mission

European mission

cockroach
2007

silkworm
2003

beetle
1995

scorpion
2007

newt
1985

bee
2003

gecko
2014

jellyfish
1991

cricket
1998

tardigrade
(water bear)
2007

1981

1987

1993

ant
2003

1999

gerbil
2007

2005

These are a few of the creatures
that have made the trip into space.
Some animals were sent on more
than one mission—the date shows
when an animal first left Earth.

2011

Solar system oceans

Scientists believe there are at least nine solar system planets, dwarf planets, or moons with liquid water oceans. These are the most likely places for life to exist in the solar system.

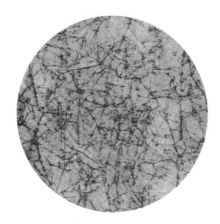

The oceans of the solar system moons are covered by a thick layer of ice. The surface of Jupiter's moon **Europa**, above, is marked by cracks in the ice.

Amount of water on solar system planets, dwarf planets, and moons

27X as much water as on Earth

4X as much water as on Earth

2X as much water as on Earth

Earth		Europa	Callisto	Ganymede

moons of Jupiter

The size of solar system moons and dwarf planets with oceans (compared to Earth)

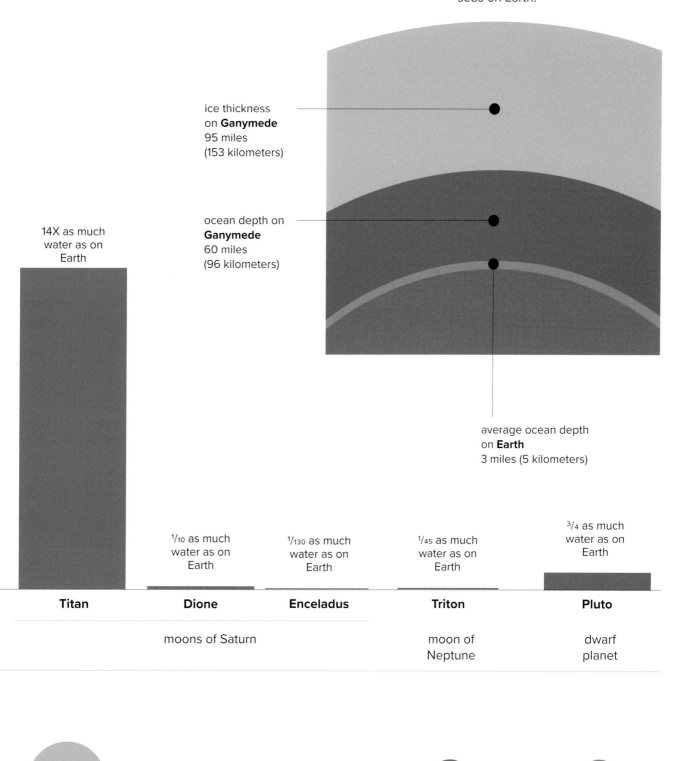

Some of these oceans contain much more water than the seas on Earth.

ice thickness on **Ganymede** 95 miles (153 kilometers)

ocean depth on **Ganymede** 60 miles (96 kilometers)

average ocean depth on **Earth** 3 miles (5 kilometers)

14X as much water as on Earth

1/10 as much water as on Earth

1/130 as much water as on Earth

1/45 as much water as on Earth

3/4 as much water as on Earth

Titan

Dione

Enceladus

Triton

Pluto

moons of Saturn

moon of Neptune

dwarf planet

Danger from space

Sometimes an asteroid or comet crashes into Earth. Even a small asteroid can cause serious damage. A large one can threaten most life on our planet. Fortunately, these collisions are rare.

Impacts	How big is the object?	About how often does one hit Earth?	What are the effects of the impact?*
	150 feet (46 meters)	1,000 years	destroys a small city
	330 feet (100 meters)	5,000 years	destroys a large city
	½ mile (800 meters)	250,000 years	destroys a small country; some worldwide climate effects
	6 miles (10 kilometers)	100 million years	global destruction, mass extinctions of plants and animals

An asteroid six miles (10 kilometers) across crashed into Earth 66 million years ago. It was probably responsible for killing off the dinosaurs.

The effects of an impact vary with the speed, angle of entry, and composition of an asteroid or comet.

Is there life elsewhere in the solar system?

So far, Earth is the only place we know of where life exists. But there are other places in the solar system that could support life. Here are a few of the most interesting.

Life as we know it needs liquid water to exist. Water can probably be found on several moons and at least one other planet.

Mars
Some scientists think this is the most likely place to find life beyond Earth.

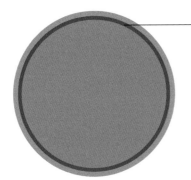

Liquid water beneath the surface could be home to microscopic organisms.

Enceladus
(moon of Saturn)

**Ganymede
Callisto
Europa**
(moons of Jupiter)

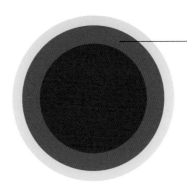

These moons have liquid oceans beneath a thick layer of ice. It's possible life could exist in these waters.

Two places where strange forms of life might exist without water:

Venus
The surface is too hot for life. But high above the surface, drifting microbes might feed on chemicals in the clouds.

Titan
This moon of Saturn has rain, rivers, and lakes. But the liquid isn't water—it's similar to the gas we put into our cars.

What would life on other moons or planets look like?
We haven't found it, so we don't know. But there is a good chance that if life exists, it will in the form of small, simple organisms.

Perhaps life elsewhere will be similar to bacteria on Earth.

It almost certainly won't look like the aliens in movies and TV shows.

PLANET EARTH

From space, the Earth looks like a smooth blue ball. Move closer, and you'll see towering mountain peaks and rugged canyons. There are deep, dark seas, vast deserts, and huge flowing sheets of ice.

The Earth is constantly changing. Over millions of years, mountains rise, rivers change course, and continents collide. Other things happen much more quickly. In the blink of an eye, hurricanes, earthquakes, and volcanoes change the Earth in dramatic ways.

The infographics in this chapter can help us understand some of the forces that shape our planet.

Words in blue can be found in the glossary on page 154.

The Earth's surface

water

More than two-thirds of our planet's surface is covered by water.

land

water

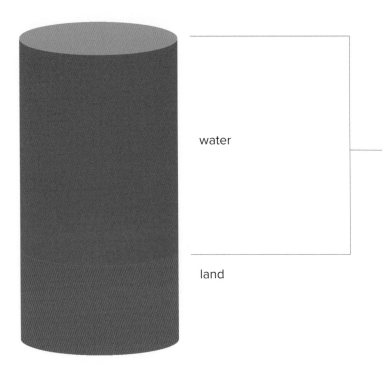

water

land

land

Human settlements cover only a small fraction of the Earth's land.

towns and cities

ice sheets and glaciers

deserts

forests and jungles

farms, pastures, and grazing areas

The thickness of the color bands shows how much of the land's surface is taken up by each environment.

But most of the Earth's water is salty.

And most of Earth's fresh water is underground or frozen.

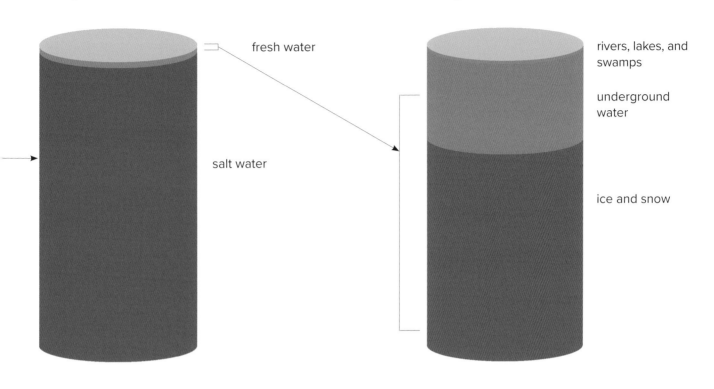

fresh water

salt water

rivers, lakes, and swamps

underground water

ice and snow

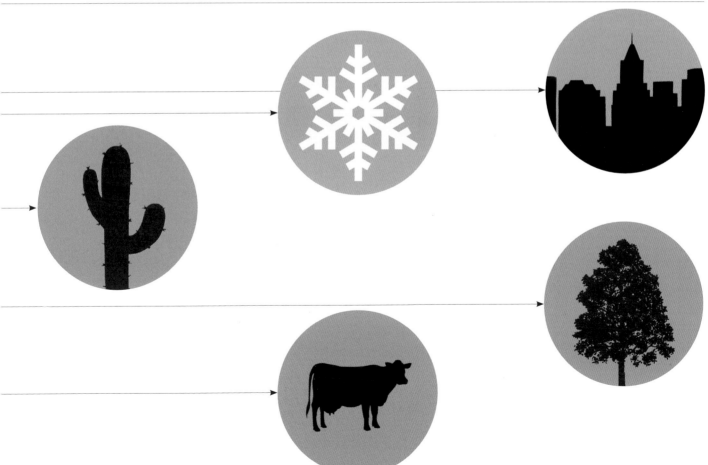

What's inside?

It is 3,960 miles (6,373 kilometers) from the surface to the center of the Earth.

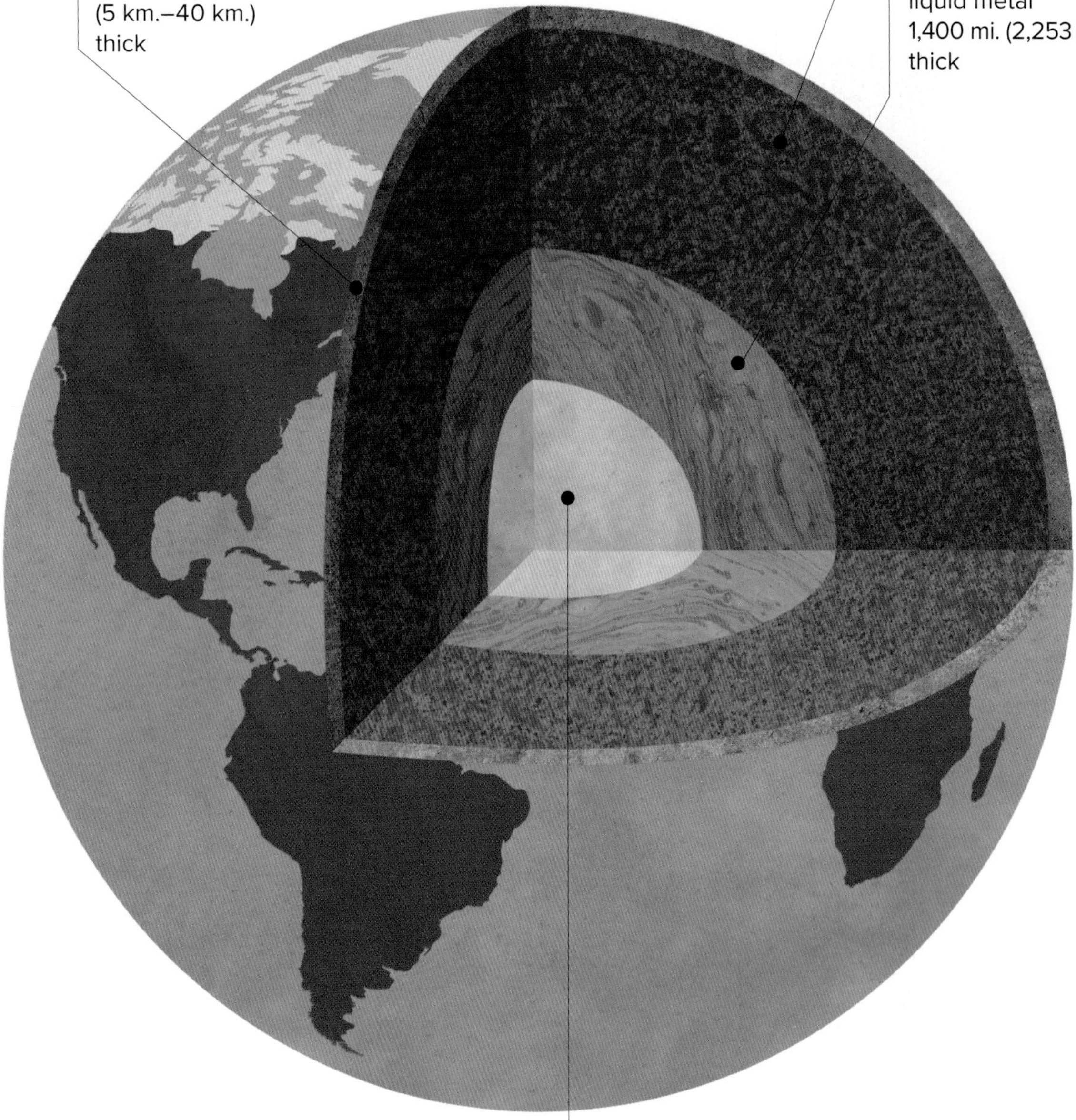

crust
solid rock
3 mi.–25 mi.*
(5 km.–40 km.)
thick

mantle
partially molten rock
1,800 mi. (2,897 km.)
thick

outer core
liquid metal
1,400 mi. (2,253 km.)
thick

inner core
solid metal
1,520 mi. (2,446 km.)
in diameter

* Throughout this chapter:
***miles** are abbreviated as mi.*
***kilometers** are abbreviated as km.*
***feet** are abbreviated as ft.*
***meters** are abbreviated as m.*

The deepest places on Earth

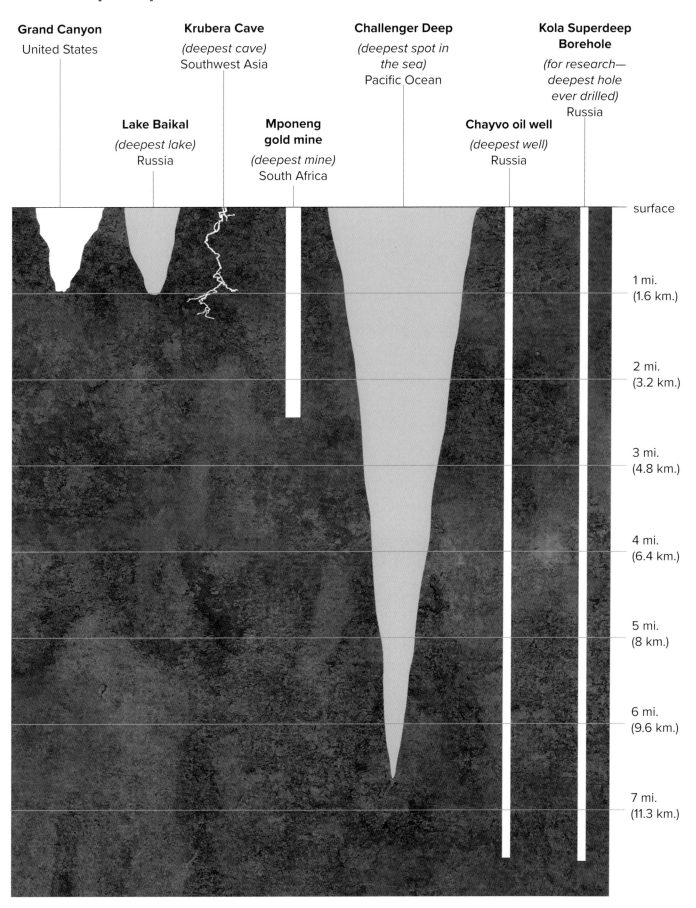

Grand Canyon
United States

Krubera Cave
(deepest cave)
Southwest Asia

Lake Baikal
(deepest lake)
Russia

Mponeng gold mine
(deepest mine)
South Africa

Challenger Deep
(deepest spot in the sea)
Pacific Ocean

Chayvo oil well
(deepest well)
Russia

Kola Superdeep Borehole
(for research— deepest hole ever drilled)
Russia

surface

1 mi. (1.6 km.)

2 mi. (3.2 km.)

3 mi. (4.8 km.)

4 mi. (6.4 km.)

5 mi. (8 km.)

6 mi. (9.6 km.)

7 mi. (11.3 km.)

Mountains

These are the highest mountain peaks on each of the seven continents.

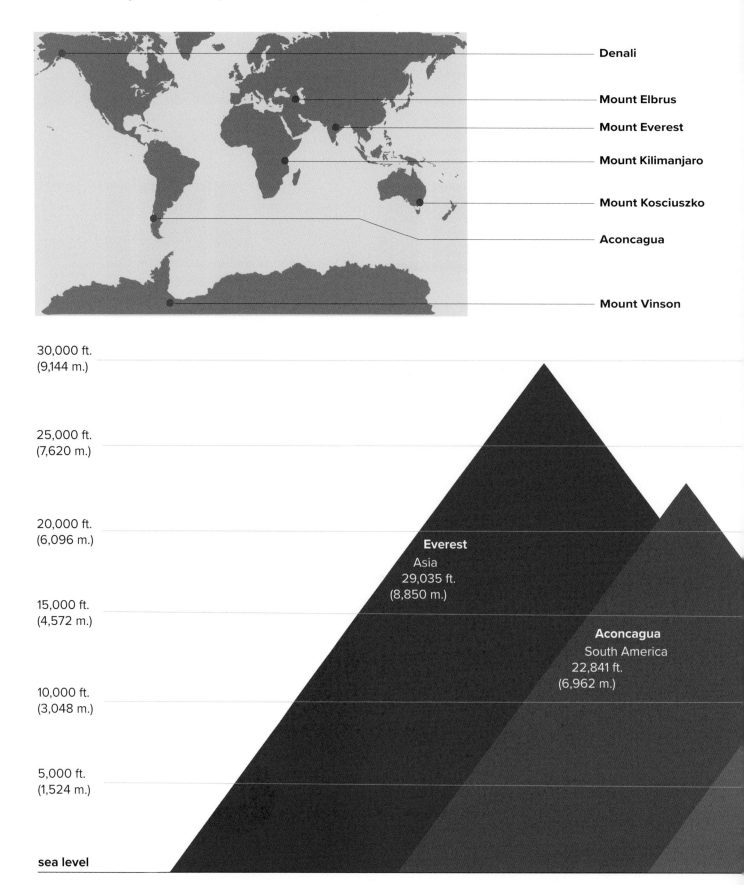

Denali

Mount Elbrus

Mount Everest

Mount Kilimanjaro

Mount Kosciuszko

Aconcagua

Mount Vinson

30,000 ft.
(9,144 m.)

25,000 ft.
(7,620 m.)

20,000 ft.
(6,096 m.)

15,000 ft.
(4,572 m.)

10,000 ft.
(3,048 m.)

5,000 ft.
(1,524 m.)

sea level

Everest
Asia
29,035 ft.
(8,850 m.)

Aconcagua
South America
22,841 ft.
(6,962 m.)

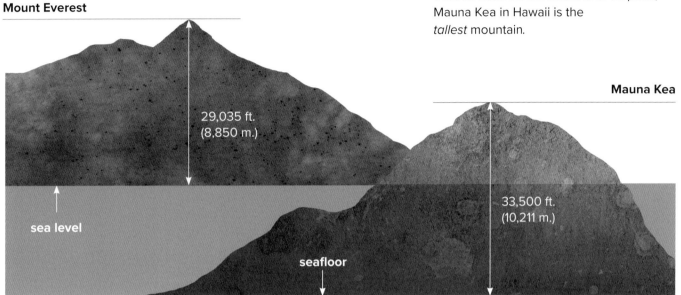

Mount Everest

29,035 ft.
(8,850 m.)

sea level

seafloor

The tallest mountain

Mount Everest, in Asia, is the *highest* mountain (above sea level). But measured from its base on the seafloor to its peak, Mauna Kea in Hawaii is the *tallest* mountain.

Mauna Kea

33,500 ft.
(10,211 m.)

In 2015, the name *Mount McKinley* was changed to *Denali,* a name used by the native people who live in the area.

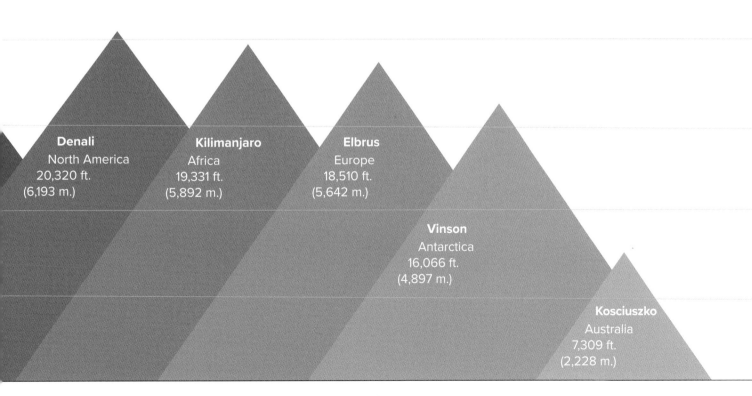

Denali
North America
20,320 ft.
(6,193 m.)

Kilimanjaro
Africa
19,331 ft.
(5,892 m.)

Elbrus
Europe
18,510 ft.
(5,642 m.)

Vinson
Antarctica
16,066 ft.
(4,897 m.)

Kosciuszko
Australia
7,309 ft.
(2,228 m.)

Rivers and lakes

Fresh water on the Earth's surface (not including ice and snow)

rivers

swamps and marshes

lakes

Length of four of the world's great rivers

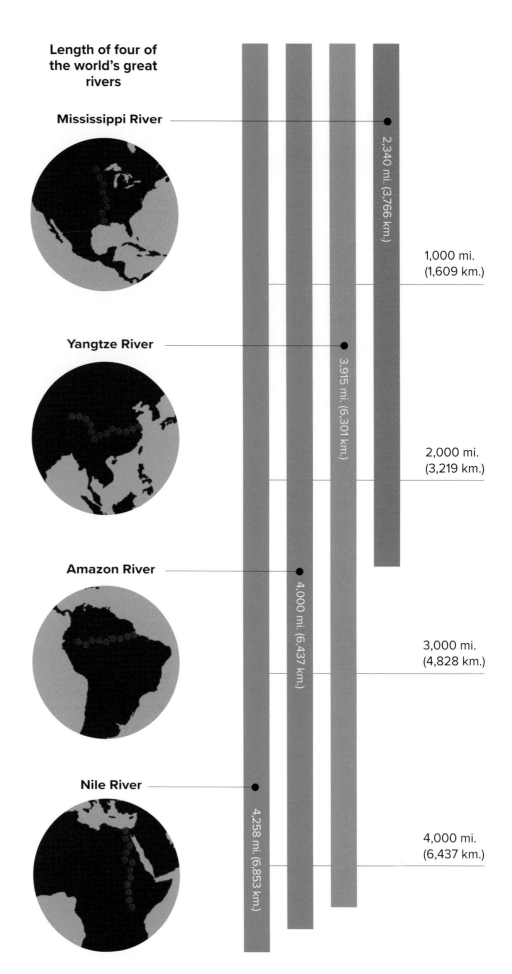

Mississippi River

2,340 mi. (3,766 km.)

Yangtze River

3,915 mi. (6,301 km.)

Amazon River

4,000 mi. (6,437 km.)

Nile River

4,258 mi. (6,853 km.)

1,000 mi. (1,609 km.)

2,000 mi. (3,219 km.)

3,000 mi. (4,828 km.)

4,000 mi. (6,437 km.)

Four of the world's largest lakes

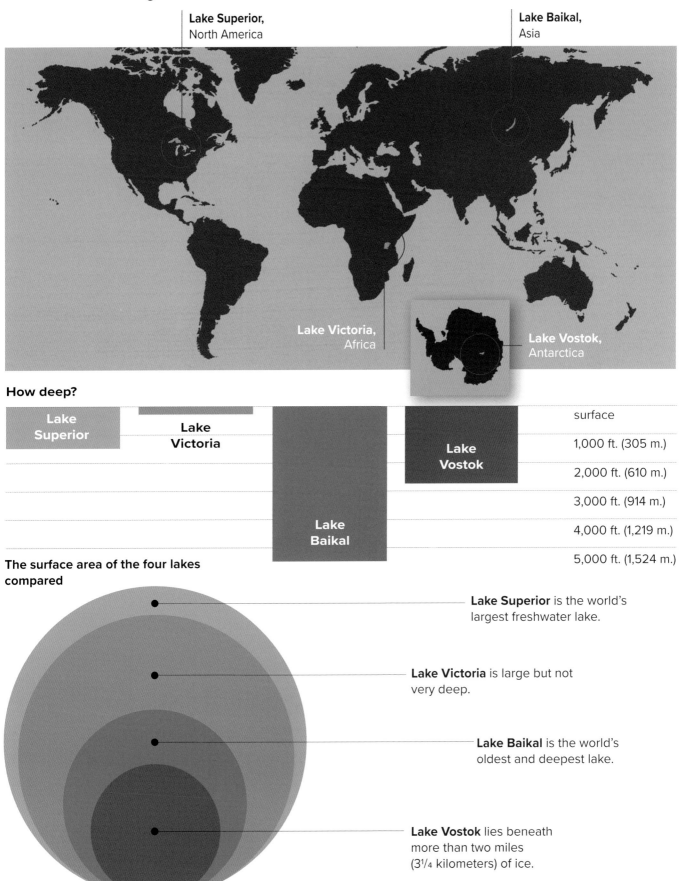

Lake Superior,
North America

Lake Baikal,
Asia

Lake Victoria,
Africa

Lake Vostok,
Antarctica

How deep?

Lake Superior	
Lake Victoria	surface
Lake Vostok	1,000 ft. (305 m.)
	2,000 ft. (610 m.)
	3,000 ft. (914 m.)
Lake Baikal	4,000 ft. (1,219 m.)
	5,000 ft. (1,524 m.)

The surface area of the four lakes compared

Lake Superior is the world's largest freshwater lake.

Lake Victoria is large but not very deep.

Lake Baikal is the world's oldest and deepest lake.

Lake Vostok lies beneath more than two miles (3¼ kilometers) of ice.

49

Ice and snow

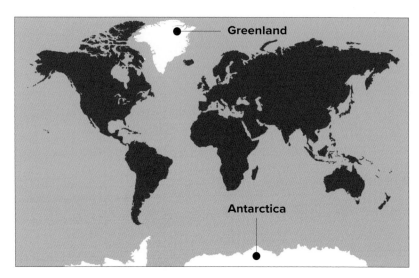

The thick layers of ice that cover most of Greenland and Antarctica are called ice caps.

In some places, the ice covering Antarctica is more than three miles (5 kilometers) thick.

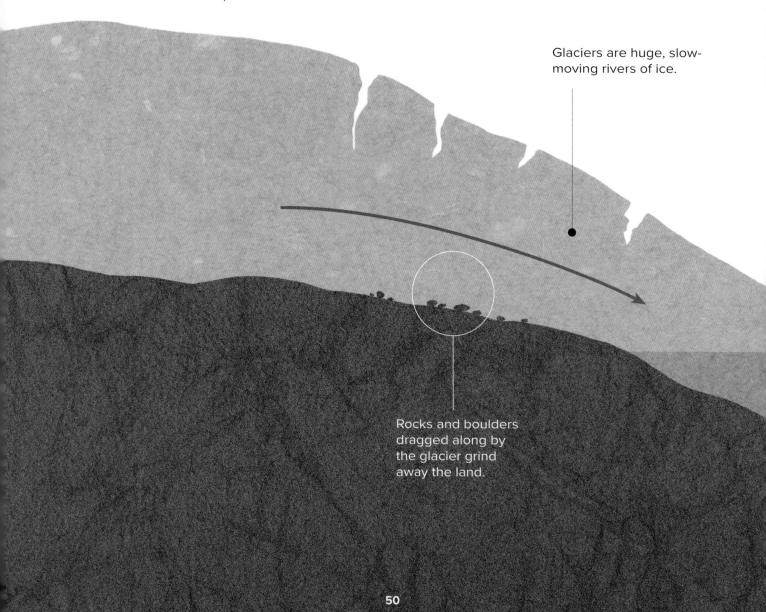

Glaciers are huge, slow-moving rivers of ice.

Rocks and boulders dragged along by the glacier grind away the land.

Glaciers and ice caps form when snow builds up year after year. The weight of the snow turns the bottom layers of the snowpack into ice.

Most of the fresh water on the Earth's surface is frozen.

A speedy glacier moves about as fast as a snail crawls.

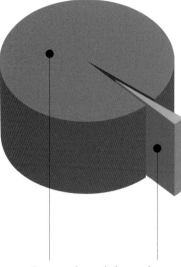

ice and snow

lakes, rivers, and marshes

Most of an iceberg lies below the water's surface.

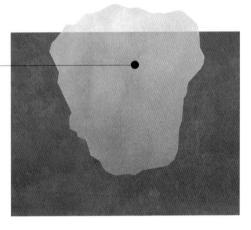

When a glacier reaches the sea, chunks of ice break off and form icebergs.

floating ice sheet

Oceans

Most of the ocean is in perpetual darkness.

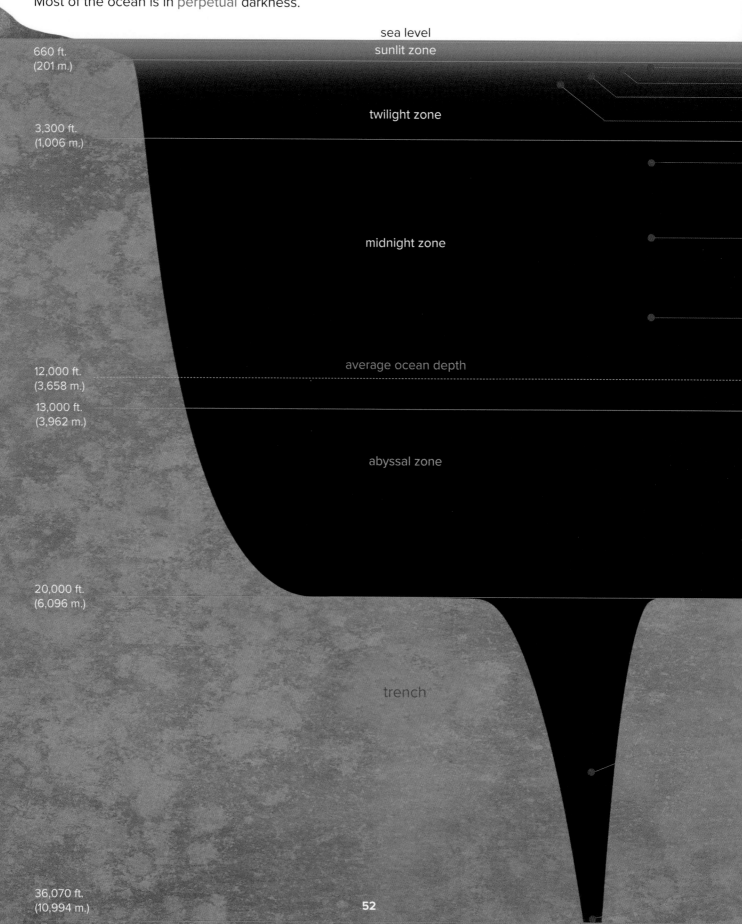

sea level

660 ft.
(201 m.)

sunlit zone

twilight zone

3,300 ft.
(1,006 m.)

midnight zone

average ocean depth

12,000 ft.
(3,658 m.)

13,000 ft.
(3,962 m.)

abyssal zone

20,000 ft.
(6,096 m.)

trench

36,070 ft.
(10,994 m.)

How deep?
Some record dives
(illustrations not to scale)

murre
deepest diving
flying bird
690 ft.
(210 m.)

**human free-diving
record**
without air tanks
702 ft.
(214 m.)

emperor penguin
deepest diving bird
1,755 ft.
(535 m.)

scuba diving
record
1,090 ft.
(332 m.)

leatherback turtle
deepest diving turtle
4,200 ft.
(1,280 m.)

sperm whale
7,380 ft.
(2,250 m.)

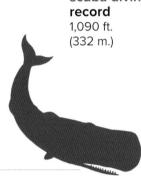

**Cuvier's beaked
whale**
deepest diving
mammal
9,816 ft.
(2,992 m.)

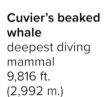

deepsea snailfish
deepest fish
26,247 ft.
(8,000 m.)

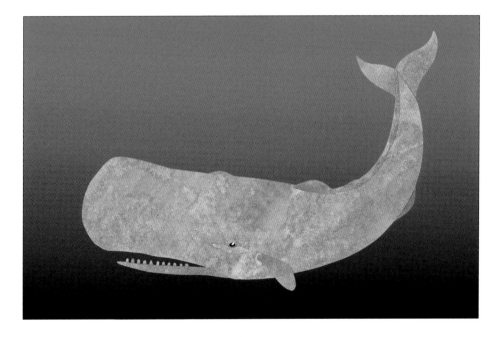

Challenger Deep
In the Mariana Trench,
the deepest spot
in the ocean

**Deepsea
Challenger**
submersible
35,756 ft.
(10,898 m.)

Earth's extremes

Highest and lowest temperatures

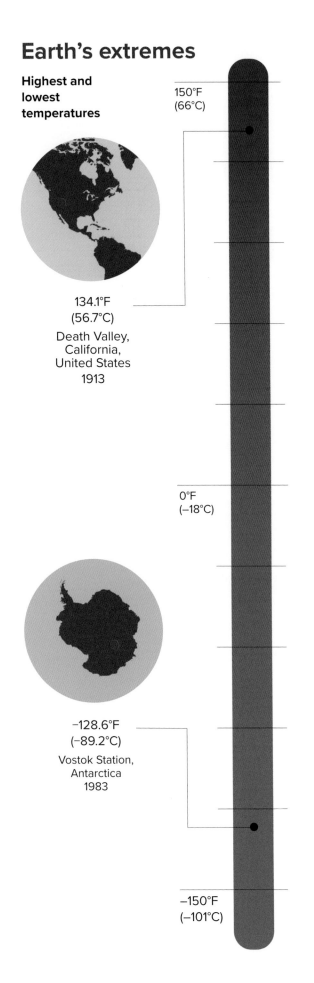

150°F (66°C)

134.1°F (56.7°C)

Death Valley, California, United States 1913

0°F (−18°C)

−128.6°F (−89.2°C)

Vostok Station, Antarctica 1983

−150°F (−101°C)

Windiest place on earth

maximum wind speed recorded here: 231 mph (372 kph)

Mount Washington, New Hampshire, United States 1934

Largest hailstone

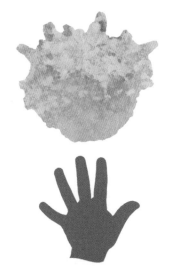

8 in. (20 cm.) in diameter

South Dakota, United States 2010

Rainfall records

467 in.
(1,186 cm.)

highest
average annual
rainfall

Meghalaya,
India

most rainfall in
24 hours

Reunion Island,
Indian Ocean
1966

72 in.
(183 cm.)

Snowfall records

1,140 in.
(2,895 cm.)

most snow in one year

Mount Baker,
Washington,
United States
1998–1999

most snow in
24 hours

Capracotta,
Italy
2015

101 in.
(257 cm.)

Driest places on Earth

Atacama Desert,
Chile,
South America

About 8/100 of
an inch (2 mm.)
of rain falls in
a year.

Dry Valleys,
Antarctica

No rain has fallen
for thousands
of years.

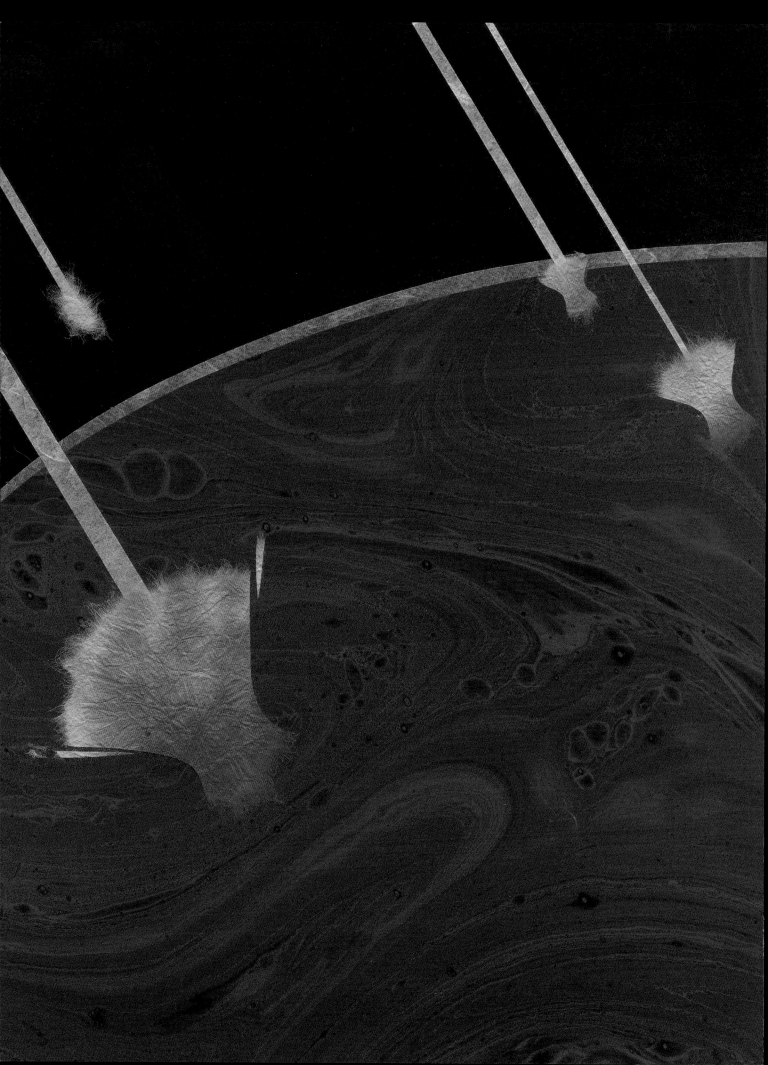

HISTORY OF THE EARTH

The Earth formed more than 4½ billion years ago from a disk of dust and debris circling the Sun. For a long time the planet was a seething ball of molten rock. Its surface was bombarded by asteroids and comets, and its atmosphere was a soup of poisonous gasses.

The story of life on Earth is one of constant destruction, renewal, and change. Beginning with a single-celled organism that appeared more than 3½ billion years ago, life has taken on an astounding number of forms. Over and over, living things have grown more and more diverse, only to experience some catastrophe— severe climate change, massive volcanic eruptions, or the impact of a comet or asteroid—that killed off most of them. After each of these mass extinctions, millions of new organisms have gradually appeared, taking advantage of the gaps left behind.

This chapter uses infographics to look at the Earth's timeline, the changing globe, the history of the Earth in 24 hours, and a timeline of animal life on Earth.

* Words in blue can be found in the glossary on page 154.

The Earth: a timeline—part 1

1,000 MYA = one billion years ago

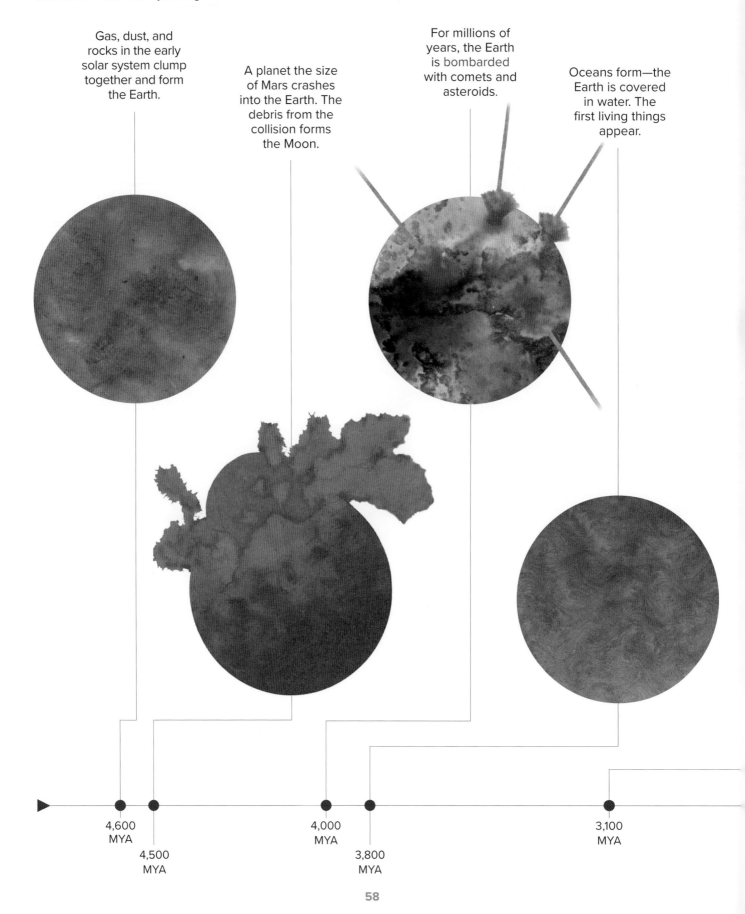

Gas, dust, and rocks in the early solar system clump together and form the Earth.

A planet the size of Mars crashes into the Earth. The debris from the collision forms the Moon.

For millions of years, the Earth is bombarded with comets and asteroids.

Oceans form—the Earth is covered in water. The first living things appear.

4,600 MYA

4,500 MYA

4,000 MYA

3,800 MYA

3,100 MYA

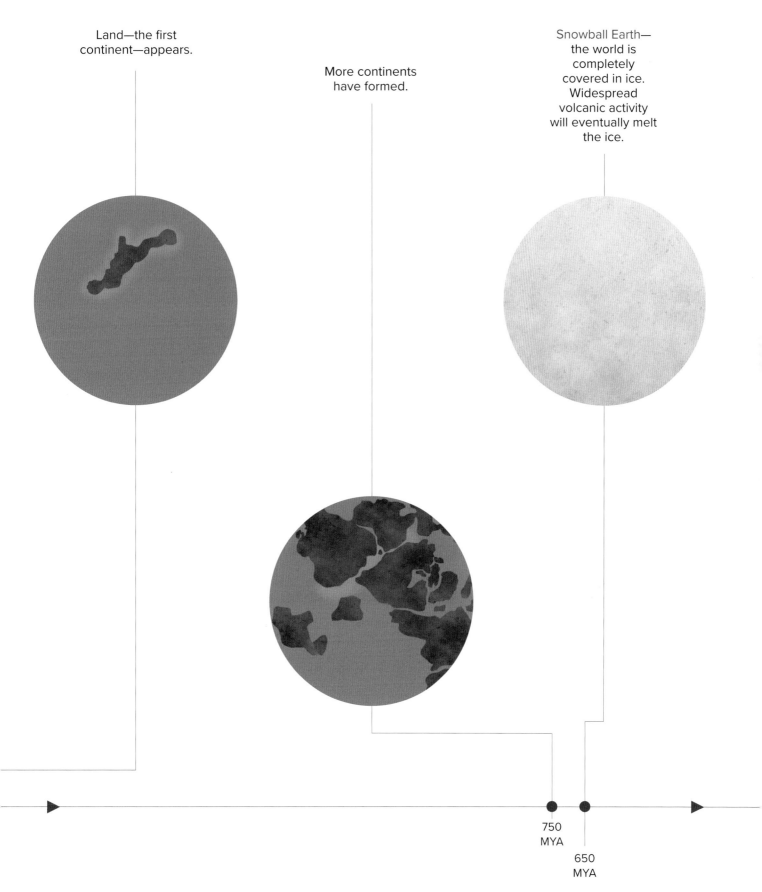

Land—the first continent—appears.

More continents have formed.

Snowball Earth—the world is completely covered in ice. Widespread volcanic activity will eventually melt the ice.

750 MYA

650 MYA

The Earth: a timeline—part 2

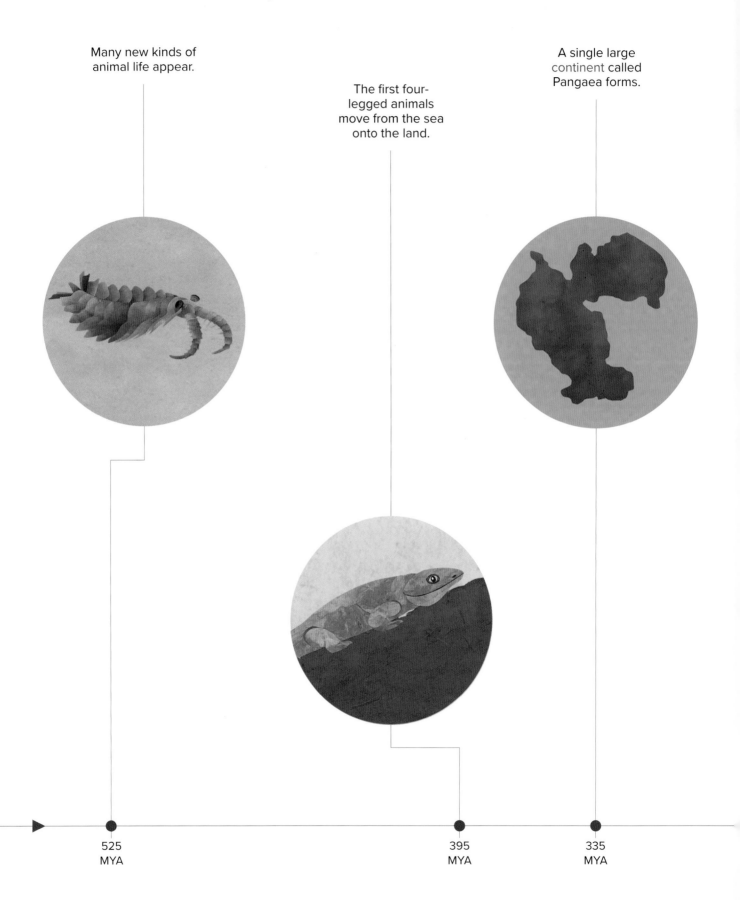

Many new kinds of
animal life appear.

The first four-
legged animals
move from the sea
onto the land.

A single large
continent called
Pangaea forms.

525
MYA

395
MYA

335
MYA

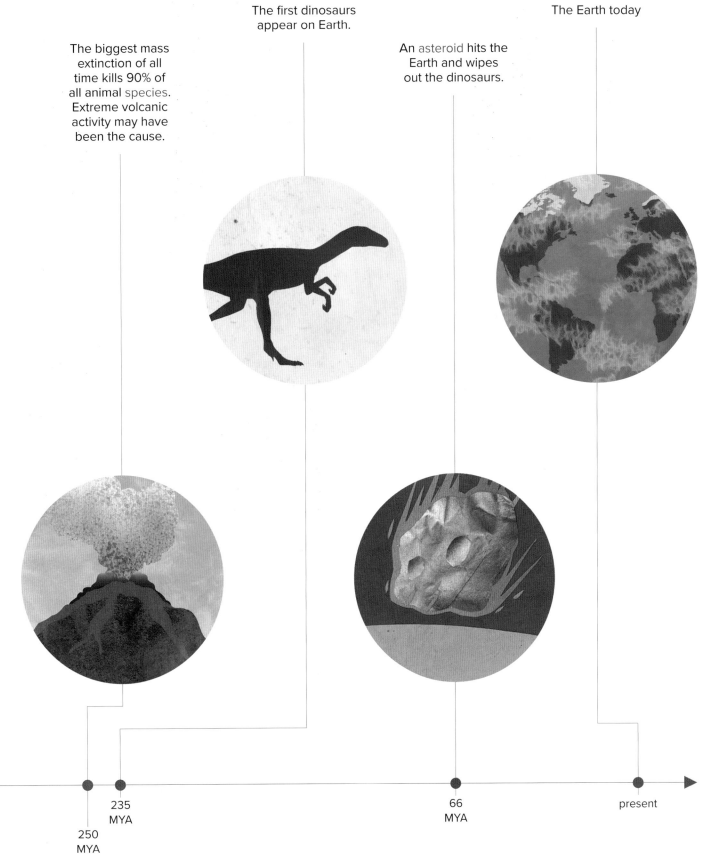

The first dinosaurs appear on Earth.

The Earth today

The biggest mass extinction of all time kills 90% of all animal species. Extreme volcanic activity may have been the cause.

An asteroid hits the Earth and wipes out the dinosaurs.

235
MYA

250
MYA

66
MYA

present

The changing globe

Over millions of years, the continents have drifted all over the globe, moving apart or crashing into each other.

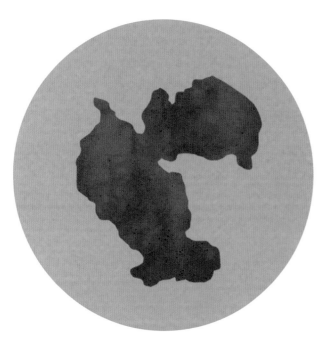

290 million years ago

150 million years ago

The motion of molten rock deep in the Earth makes the continents move.

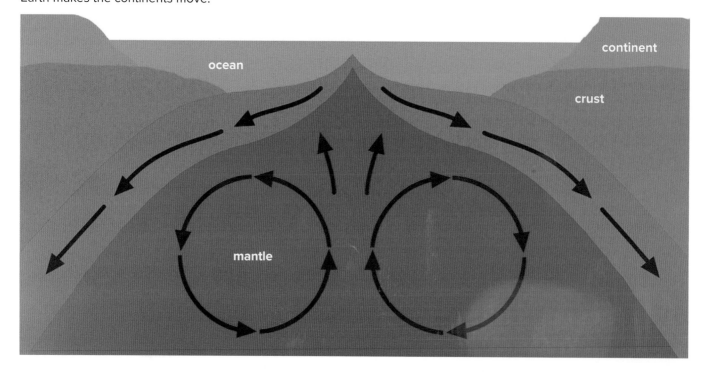

The continents move at about the same rate that your fingernails grow.

75 million years ago

Present day

Millions of years from now, the continents will once again come together and create one large landmass.

250 million years from now

A history of the Earth in 24 hours

It's not easy to get a sense of how old the
Earth really is. This timeline shows our planet's
4½-billion-year history compressed into a single
24-hour day.

(00:00)
The Earth forms.

5:00 a.m.
The first life appears.

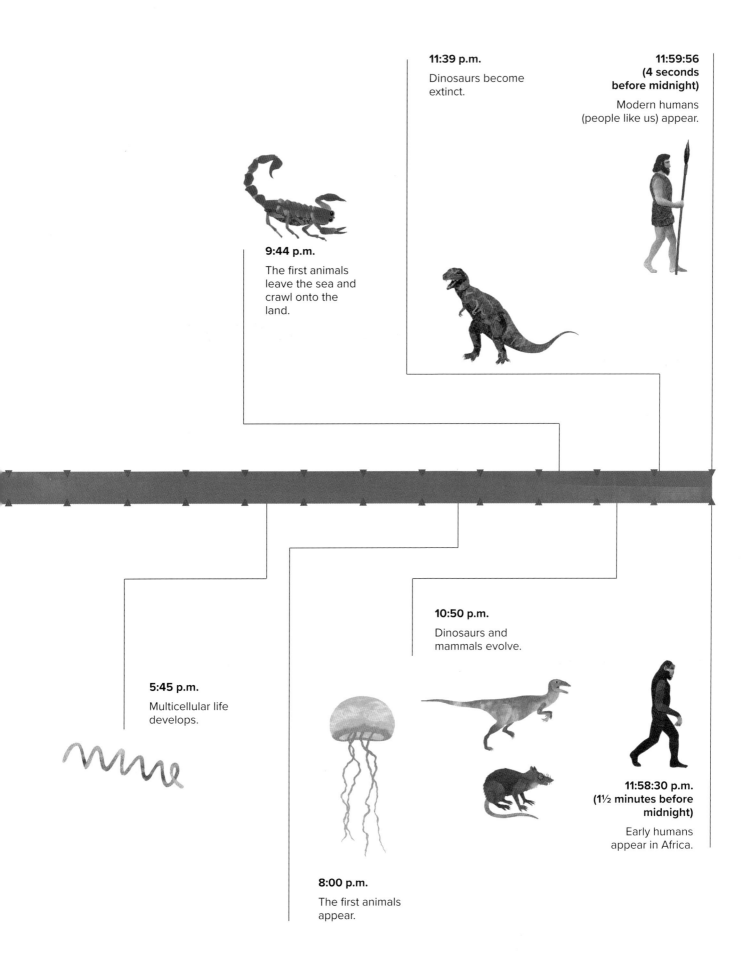

11:39 p.m.
Dinosaurs become extinct.

**11:59:56
(4 seconds before midnight)**
Modern humans (people like us) appear.

9:44 p.m.
The first animals leave the sea and crawl onto the land.

10:50 p.m.
Dinosaurs and mammals evolve.

5:45 p.m.
Multicellular life develops.

**11:58:30 p.m.
(1½ minutes before midnight)**
Early humans appear in Africa.

8:00 p.m.
The first animals appear.

A timeline of animal life on Earth

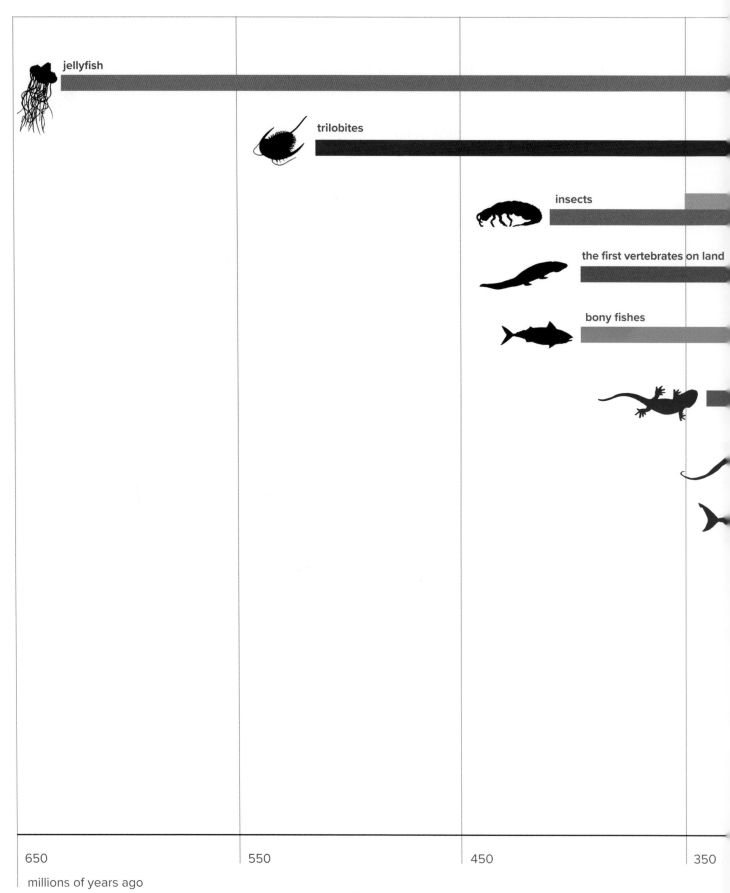

jellyfish

trilobites

insects

the first vertebrates on land

bony fishes

650   550   450   350

millions of years ago

flying insects

amphibians

reptiles

flying reptiles

sharks and rays

dinosaurs

marine mammals

mammals

modern birds

birdlike animals

upright human ancestors
and modern humans

250

150

50

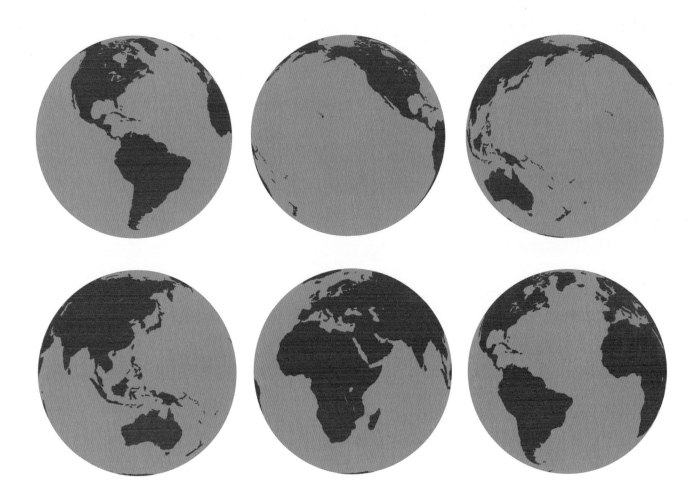

ONE DAY ON EARTH

You might be surprised at what happens in just one day. Did you know that we travel more than 1½ million miles as the Earth orbits the Sun? Or that almost 400,000 babies are born? Or that a hummingbird can fly 500 miles without taking a break?

A lot goes on in 24 hours, from the 100,000 beats of your heart to the dozens of deadly natural disasters that take place around the world.

The infographics in this chapter can help us understand some of these fascinating daily events. We'll look at how many humans are killed by animals daily, the animals we eat, some of the animals just discovered, and more.

* Words in blue can be found in the glossary on page 154.

How far do we travel in 24 hours as we go along for the ride?

The Earth is spinning and moving through space, and we move with it.

A person standing on the equator travels 25,000 miles (40,233 kilometers) around the center of the Earth as the planet rotates.

The Earth is spinning, but we don't feel its motion. Instead, it looks to us like the Sun, Moon, and stars are moving across the sky.

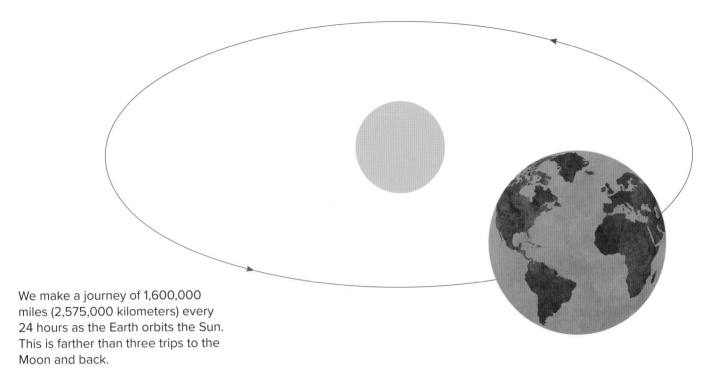

We make a journey of 1,600,000 miles (2,575,000 kilometers) every 24 hours as the Earth orbits the Sun. This is farther than three trips to the Moon and back.

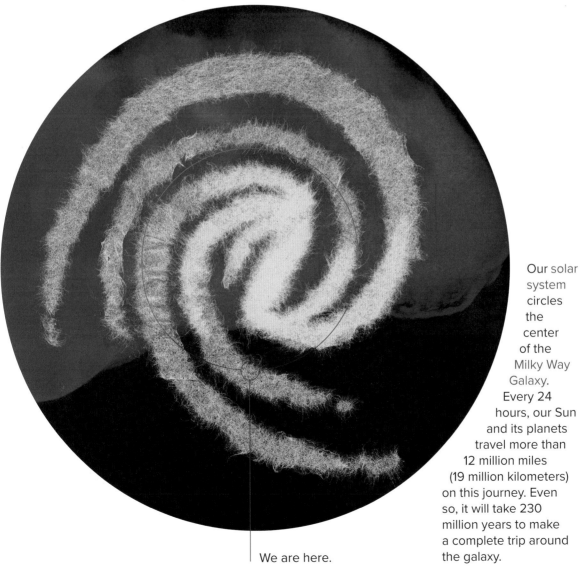

We are here.

Our solar system circles the center of the Milky Way Galaxy. Every 24 hours, our Sun and its planets travel more than 12 million miles (19 million kilometers) on this journey. Even so, it will take 230 million years to make a complete trip around the galaxy.

A 24-hour body

Every day, our bodies constantly pump blood, breathe air, shed millions of cells, and do many other things that we rarely notice.

Most people lose 50 to 100 hairs from their head each day.

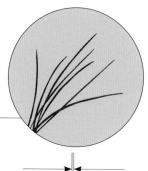

The space between the lines shows how much your hair grows each day.

Humans blink about 17,000 times a day.

Each of us produces up to 48 ounces (1½ liters) of urine, or pee, a day.

Humans eat an average of four pounds (1,814 grams) of food a day.

An adult human heart beats about 100,000 times a day, and pumps enough blood to fill 32 55-gallon (208-liter) barrels.

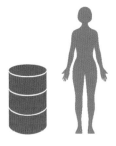

A 55-gallon barrel compared to an adult woman

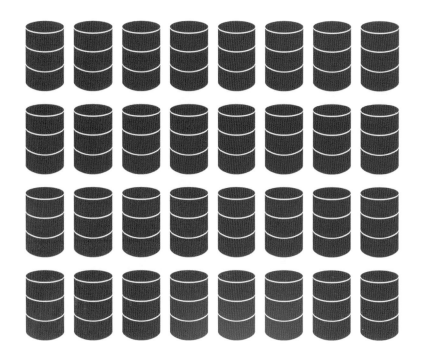

We shed about 500 million skin cells every day.

An average person takes 20,000 breaths each day. They move enough air in and out of their lungs to fill a balloon more than nine feet (2³/₄ meters) in diameter.

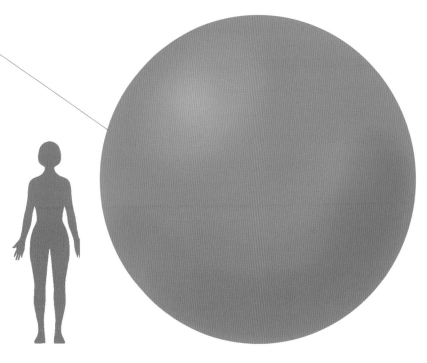

New life—and Earth

How many people are born each day?
And how many people die?

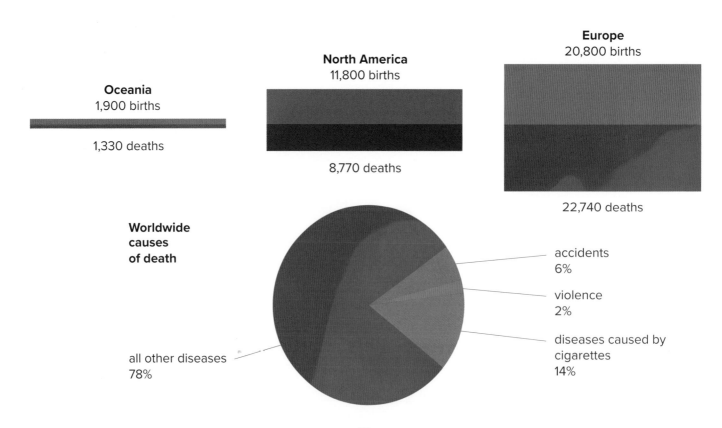

Oceania
1,900 births

1,330 deaths

North America
11,800 births

8,770 deaths

Europe
20,800 births

22,740 deaths

Worldwide causes of death

all other diseases
78%

accidents
6%

violence
2%

diseases caused by cigarettes
14%

In Europe, where the median age is 43, there are more deaths than births. In Africa, however, the median age is less than 20. On that continent, there are many more births than deaths.

Asia
202,190 births

Africa
118,360 births

Latin America
28,770 births

11,340 deaths

29,490 deaths

87,670 deaths

Around the world, approximately 384,000 babies are born every day and 161,000 people die (2020 totals).

Daily disasters

Earthquakes, tornadoes, and other dramatic natural events are unpredictable. But they happen somewhere on Earth every day.

small earthquakes
(magnitude 2.5 or less)

2,500 a day

How many earthquakes occur each day?

moderate earthquakes
(magnitude 5.4 to 6.0)

4 a day

minor earthquakes
(magnitude 2.5 to 5.4)

80 a day

In these earthquakes, shaking is quite noticeable. There can be slight damage to buildings.

These quakes are not as strong, but are usually noticeable. Objects may fall off shelves.

These small quakes are detected by scientific instruments. They are not usually felt by people.

How many tornadoes occur daily?

On average, there are four tornadoes a day somewhere in the world.
Eighty percent of all tornadoes form in the United States and Canada.

Lightning strikes

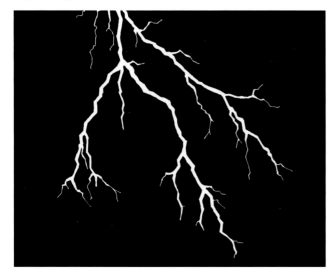

Lightning strikes somewhere on Earth
almost four million times a day.

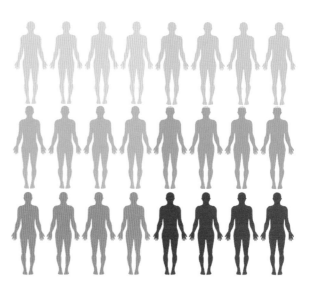

Between four and twenty-four people are killed by
lightning every day.

How many volcanic eruptions take place in a day?

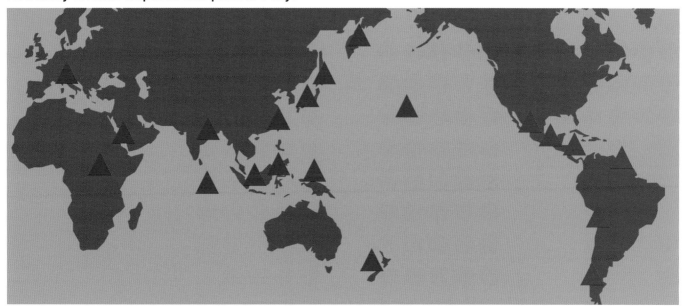

Worldwide, an average of 20 volcanoes erupt each day.

How many humans are killed by animals in a day?

People kill billions of animals every day, mostly for food. But there are some animals that kill people. Sometimes they kill humans for food. But most human deaths happen when creatures defend themselves or transmit deadly diseases.

crocodile
3 people

tsetse fly
25 people

roundworm
5 people

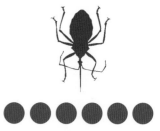

assassin bug
30 people

dog
150 people

 each circle = 5 human deaths

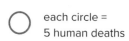 physical injury

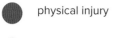 disease

 venom

freshwater snail
275 people

snake
275 people

Sharks are one of the most feared animals on earth, but they kill only about one person every month or two.

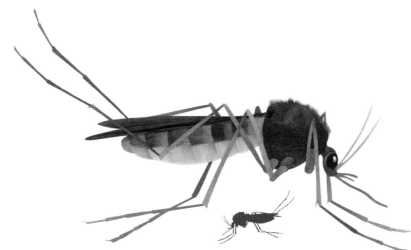

Humans are the second most deadly animal, killing more than 1,300 other humans every day.

mosquito
2,500 people

The animals we eat

Every day, people around the world eat billions of animals. Each silhouette on this page represents one million animals.

sheep
1¹/₂ million

goats
1¹/₅ million

geese
2 million

pigs
4 million

turkeys
2 million

ducks
11 million

rabbits
3 million

cows
800,000

We eat so many chickens and fish that a different scale is needed for these creatures. Each silhouette on this page represents 100 million animals eaten daily.

chickens
180 million

farmed fish
300 million

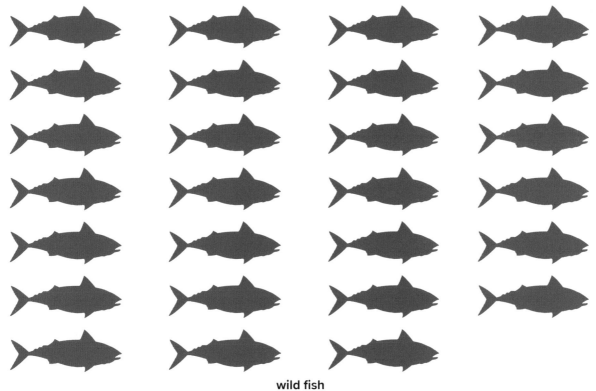

wild fish
2,700 million

Just discovered

Millions of organisms are still unknown to science. The plants and animals shown here weren't found on the same day. But an average of 50 new species are named each day.

A new kind of **leaf-tailed gecko** found in Australia

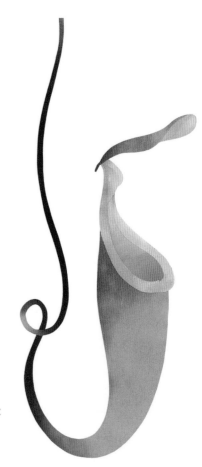

A previously unknown species of **pitcher plant** that grows in Cambodia

A **cave-dwelling beetle** from China

The **olinguito**, a South American mammal

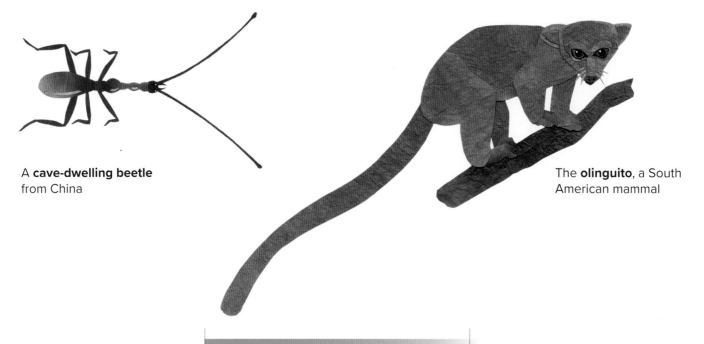

new species discovered in one day

species that go extinct in one day

| number of species | 50 | 100 |

Gone forever

These plants and animal didn't become extinct at the same time. But an estimated 150–200 species vanish every 24 hours.

The **Spix's macaw** was native to Brazil. (Extinct in the wild in 2000)

This **maidenhair fern** grew in China. (Extinct in 2004)

The **scimitar-horned oryx** lived in North Africa. (Probably extinct in the wild in 1980)

When he died, Lonely George was the last **Hawaiian tree snail** of his kind. (Extinct in 2019)

The **West African black rhinoceros** was once found throughout Central Africa. (Extinct in 2003)

The **golden toad** lived in the mountains of Costa Rica. (Extinct in 2004)

150

200

250

Daily energy use

Most of the energy we use comes from fossil fuels, including coal, oil, and natural gas. Burning fossil fuels—especially coal—releases gases that are causing our climate to heat up. These fuels are gradually being replaced by cleaner forms of energy such as hydroelectric, wind, and solar power.

The amount of coal burned around the world every day compared to a 10-story building.

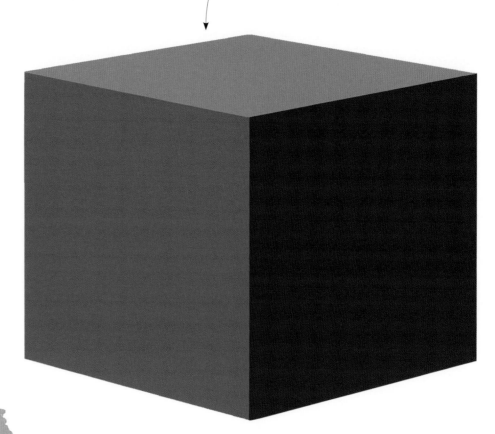

This building is more than 100 feet (30 meters) tall.

Almost all of our energy comes from the sun.*

Wind is created by the sun heating the atmosphere. Fossil fuels release energy from sunlight that was captured and stored by plants millions of years ago. Even hydroelectric power, which is produced by water, relies on the power of the sun to create precipitation.

The coal burned daily could fill 200,000 train cars.

* The exceptions are nuclear energy, which relies on the decay of radioactive elements, and thermal energy, which comes from volcanic sources inside the Earth.

Around the world, people use about 95 million barrels, or four billion gallons (15 billion liters), of oil every day. This is about one-half gallon of oil per person each day.

Some countries use more oil than others.

Gallons (liters) of oil used daily per person

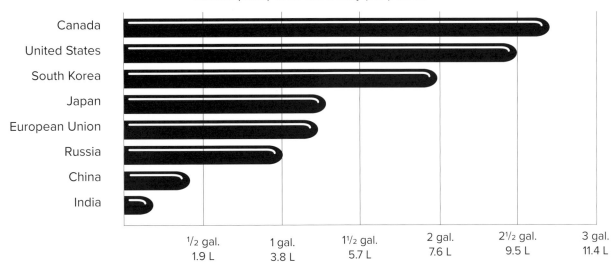

	½ gal. 1.9 L	1 gal. 3.8 L	1½ gal. 5.7 L	2 gal. 7.6 L	2½ gal. 9.5 L	3 gal. 11.4 L

Canada
United States
South Korea
Japan
European Union
Russia
China
India

The world's energy sources

When all sources of energy are combined, the world uses the energy equivalent of 280 million barrels of oil a day.

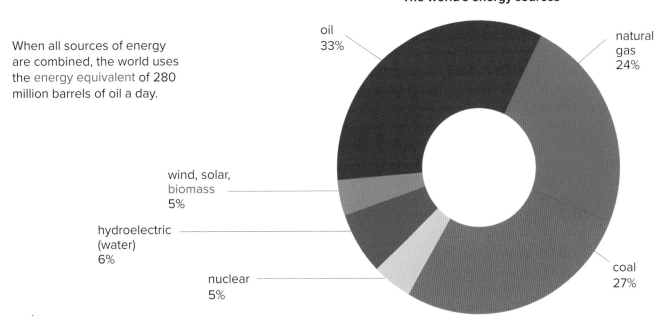

oil
33%

natural gas
24%

coal
27%

wind, solar, biomass
5%

hydroelectric (water)
6%

nuclear
5%

The modern world

Here are some surprising facts and figures about things we make, consume, and throw away—every day.

Around the world, 266,000 new cars are built.

Six thousand new books are published.

More than 15 billion cigarettes are smoked (and 27,000 people die from smoking).

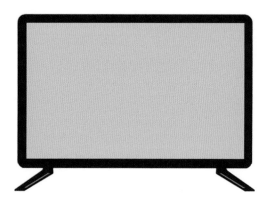

More than 580,000 new televisions are manufactured.

Almost four billion 12-ounce soft drinks are consumed.

Around 175,000 commercial flights take off (not including personal aircraft or military flights).

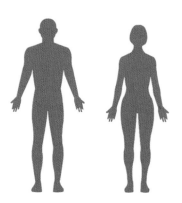

And about 12 million people fly somewhere.

Each day, 50 million pounds of plastic waste make their way into the ocean. That's the equivalent of more than two billion plastic water bottles.

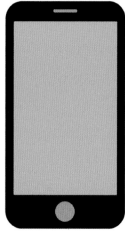

 The world's daily trash production (below) compared to a 10-story building

More than four million cell phones are sold every day.

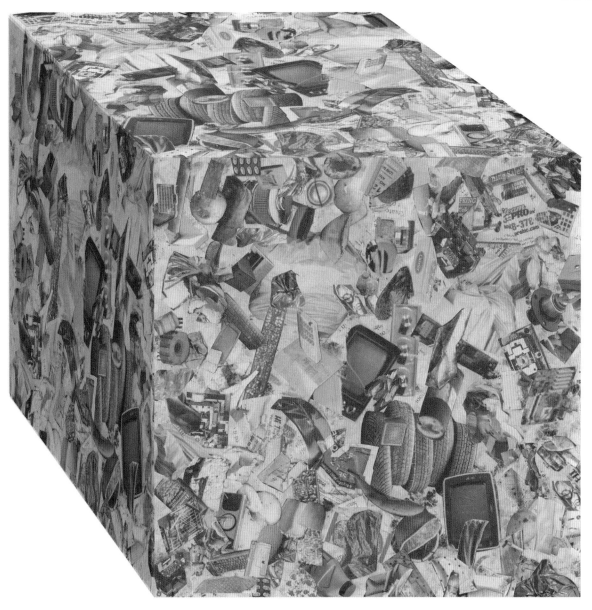

CREATURES ON EARTH

Dinosaurs ruled the Earth for more than 150 million years. Some were small, speedy, and covered with feathers. Others were huge, armor-plated beasts. There were fierce predators with terrifying teeth and claws. A gigantic plant-eating dinosaur was the largest animal to ever live on land. These amazing animals lived all over the world. Then, about 66 million years ago, almost all of them vanished. This chapter introduces the dinosaurs that are still alive today along with many other creatures we share our planet with.

Animals live almost everywhere on Earth. They can be found in scorching deserts and on polar ice caps. They survive on the tallest mountaintops and in the deepest parts of the sea. To exist in these different environments, animals have evolved an impressive range of shapes, sizes, and abilities.

The infographics in this chapter will take a look at the the animal kingdom, animal sizes, life spans, endangered animals, and animal extinction.

* Words in blue can be found in the glossary on page 154.

When did the dinosaurs live?

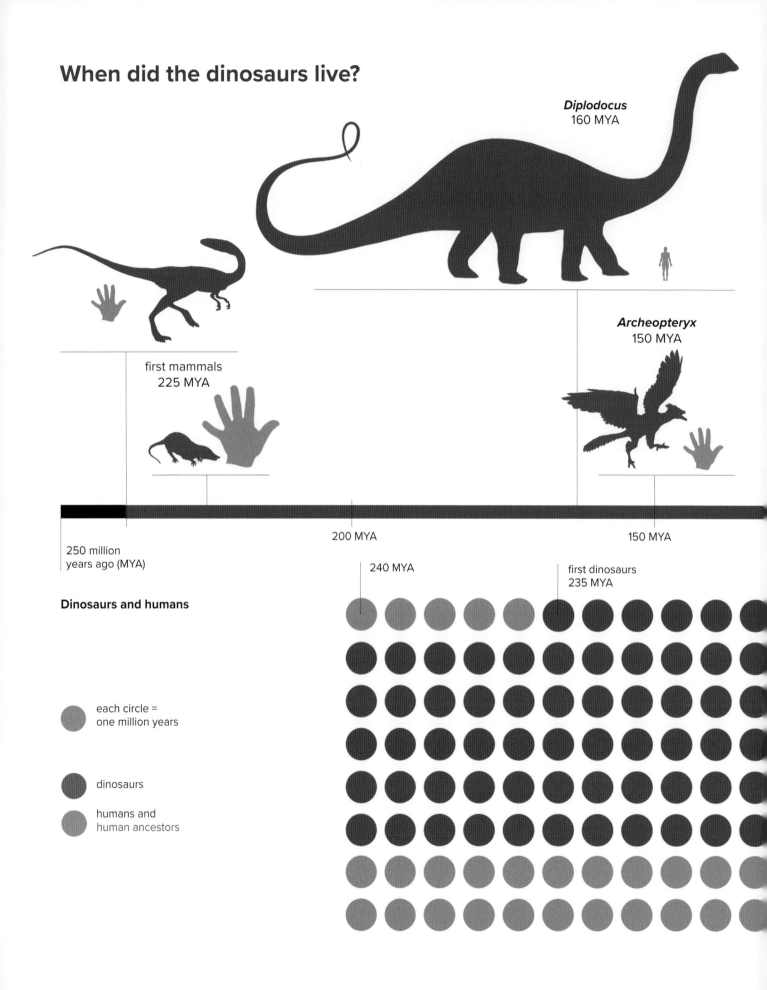

Diplodocus
160 MYA

Archeopteryx
150 MYA

first mammals
225 MYA

250 million
years ago (MYA)

200 MYA

150 MYA

240 MYA

first dinosaurs
235 MYA

Dinosaurs and humans

each circle =
one million years

dinosaurs

humans and
human ancestors

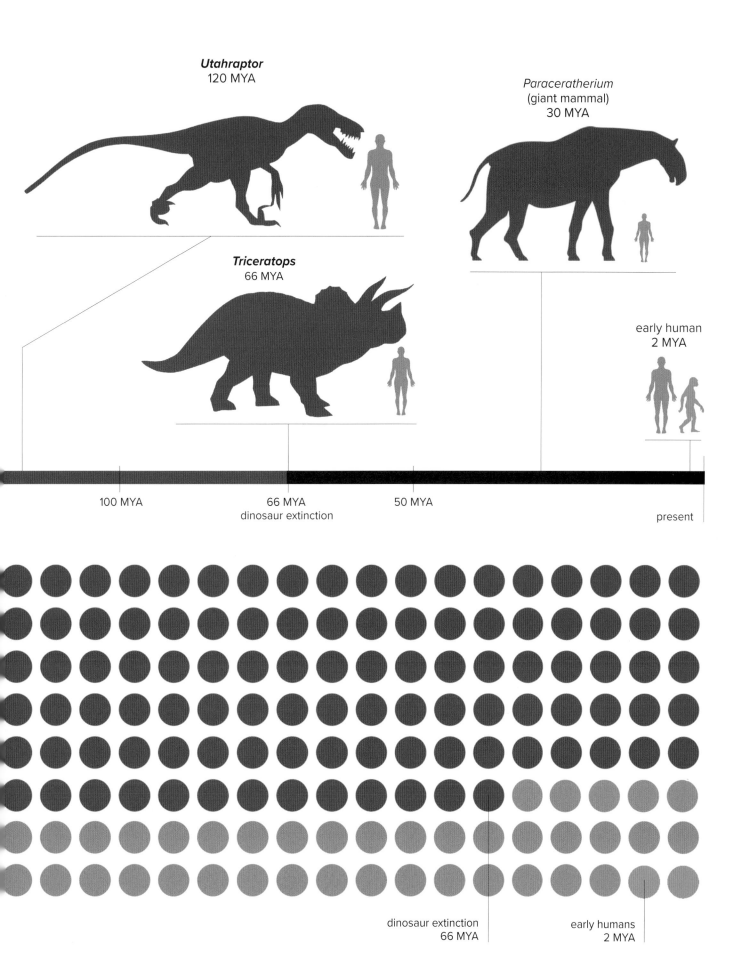

Utahraptor
120 MYA

Paraceratherium
(giant mammal)
30 MYA

Triceratops
66 MYA

early human
2 MYA

100 MYA

66 MYA
dinosaur extinction

50 MYA

present

dinosaur extinction
66 MYA

early humans
2 MYA

How big were the dinosaurs?

Dinosaurs, a few modern-day animals, and an adult human are shown at the same scale.

great white shark

Parasaurolophus

Ankylosaurus

Triceratops

grizzly bear

Tyrannosaurus rex

Therizinosaurus

blue whale

dinosaurs

modern-day animals

Stegosaurus

giraffe

Dilophosaurus

Gallimimus

Maiasaura

Archeopteryx

Spinosaurus

African elephant

saltwater crocodile

Velociraptor

Patagotitan

adult human

What killed the dinosaurs?

Sixty-six million years ago, an asteroid traveling at 20 times the speed of a bullet crashed into the Earth.

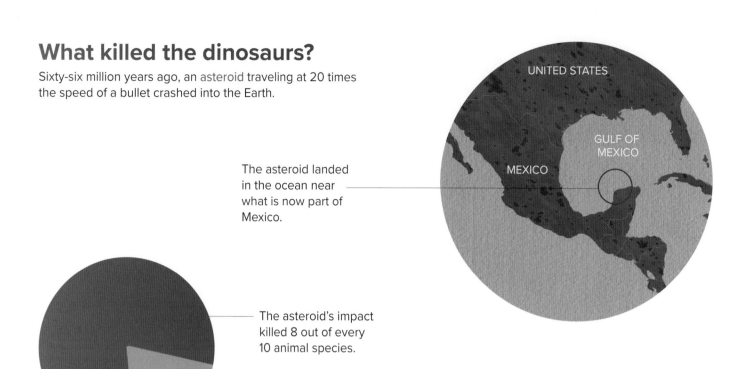

UNITED STATES

GULF OF MEXICO

MEXICO

The asteroid landed in the ocean near what is now part of Mexico.

The asteroid's impact killed 8 out of every 10 animal species.

Animal species that survived the impact

The asteroid strike caused a series of deadly events.

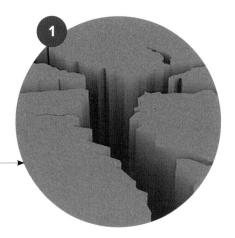

1

The shock caused powerful earthquakes.

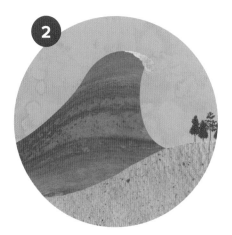

2

A tsunami as tall as a skyscraper swept across the land.

3

Red-hot debris from the impact started forest fires all over the globe.

4

The shock may have set off worldwide volcanic eruptions.

5

Dust, ash, and smoke blocked out the sunlight for years.

Massive lava flows in India at around the same time might have helped kill off the dinosaurs.

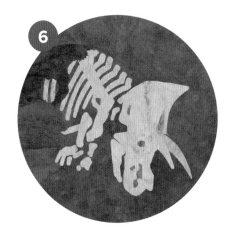

6

Without sunlight, plants could not survive. Soon the plant-eating dinosaurs died out. Without prey, the meat-eaters starved.

Living dinosaurs

Scientists tell us that birds are actually a group of dinosaurs. They survived the mass extinction that happened 66 million years ago.

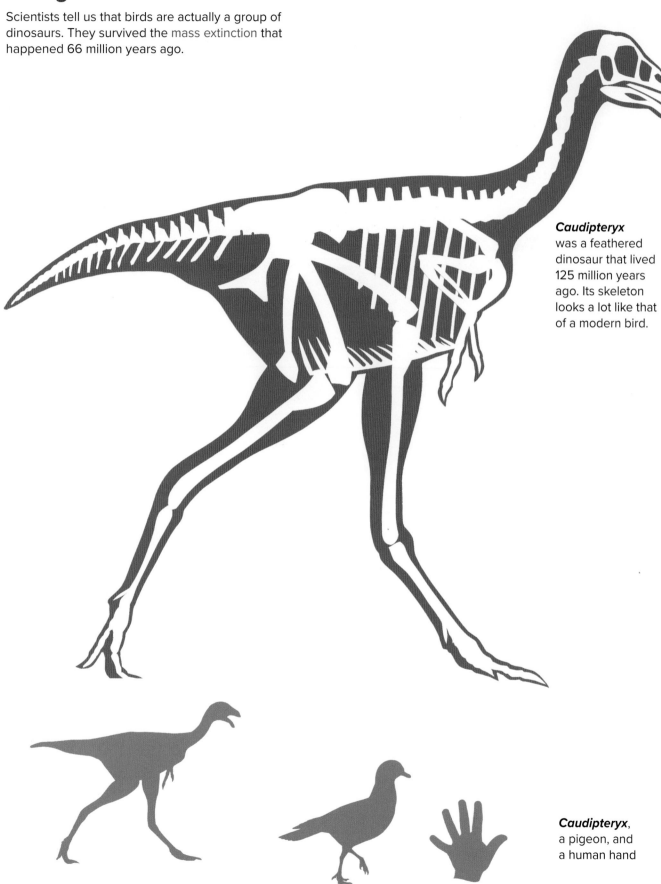

Caudipteryx was a feathered dinosaur that lived 125 million years ago. Its skeleton looks a lot like that of a modern bird.

Caudipteryx, a pigeon, and a human hand

Birds are living
dinosaurs!

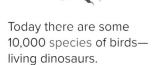

Birds evolved from
predatory dinosaurs that
could walk upright, such
as **Coelophysis**. It lived
200 million years ago.

Archeopteryx, a feathered
dinosaur, was one of the
first birds. It lived 150
million years ago.

Today there are some
10,000 species of birds—
living dinosaurs.

Animal kingdom

Fur, feathers, skin, and scales

Scientists often divide the animal world into two groups: creatures with and without backbones.

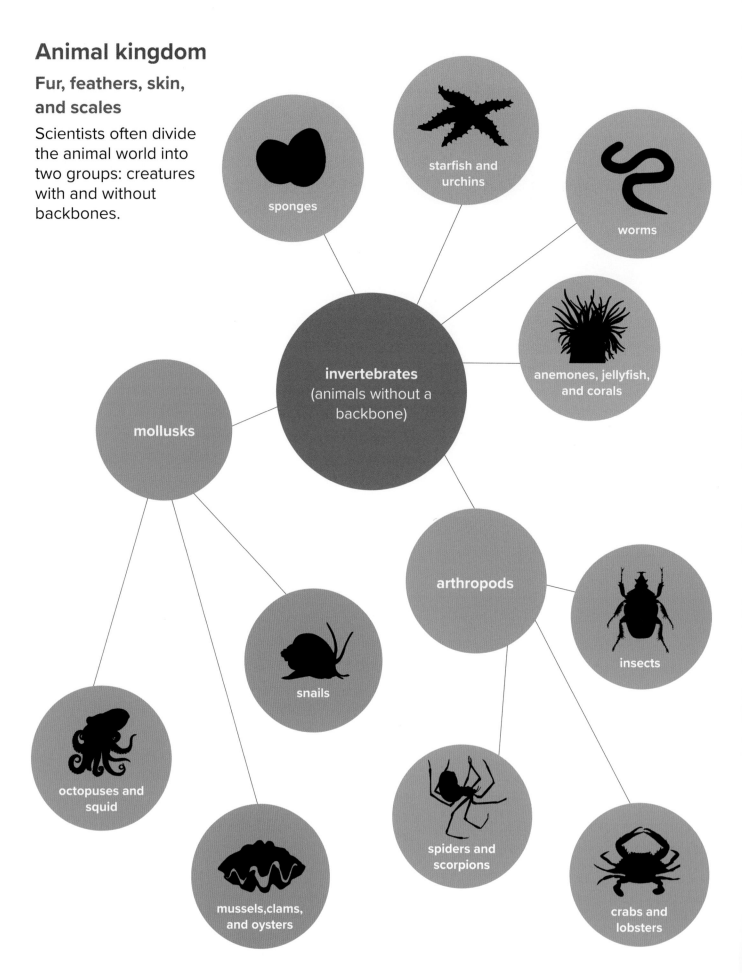

sponges

starfish and urchins

worms

invertebrates
(animals without a backbone)

anemones, jellyfish, and corals

mollusks

arthropods

snails

insects

octopuses and squid

spiders and scorpions

mussels, clams, and oysters

crabs and lobsters

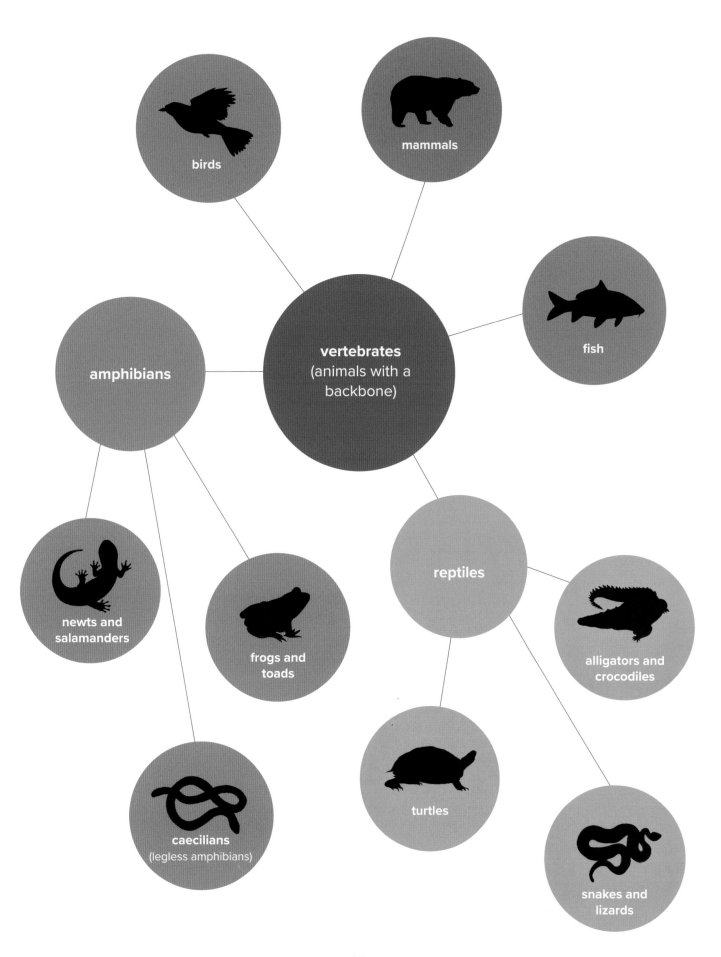

birds

mammals

vertebrates
(animals with a
backbone)

fish

amphibians

reptiles

newts and
salamanders

frogs and
toads

alligators and
crocodiles

turtles

caecilians
(legless amphibians)

snakes and
lizards

Animal species

Millions of animals

So far, well over a million species of animals have been named. Thousands of new species are discovered every year, and there are probably millions more yet to be found.

What is a species?
The basic unit that biologists use to organize the animal kingdom is the *species*. Members of a species usually look and act alike, and can mate and produce offspring.

amphibians
7,450
species

reptiles
10,000
species

birds
10,400
species

fish
32,900
species

crustaceans
67,000
species

other invertebrates
(animals without backbones)
72,000
species

mollusks
90,000
species

spiders and scorpions
102,000
species

Most animals are insects, and the largest group of insects is the beetles. Of all the animals known to science, more than one in four is a beetle.

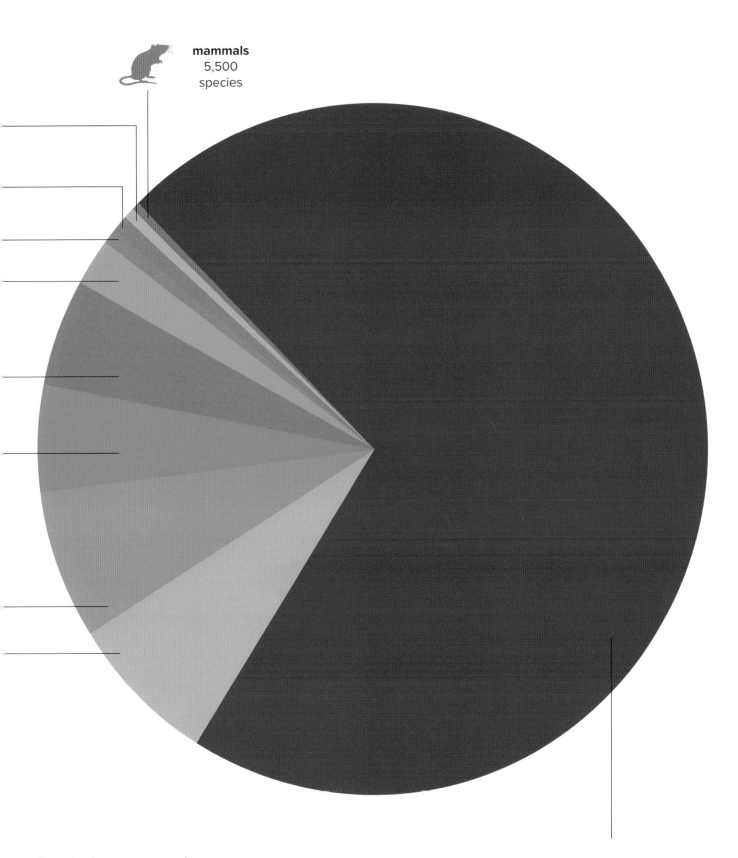

mammals
5,500
species

This pie chart represents the estimated 1,397,250 animal species that have been named. Biologists do not always agree about how many species there are, so these numbers vary from source to source.

insects
1,000,000
species

Size

Little and big

Some of the smallest and largest animals of the past and present

The **Mososaur,** a terrifying ocean predator, died out with dinosaurs 66 million years ago. The tiny **Amau frog** was discovered only recently.

 animals alive today

 extinct animals

Giants

These animals are shown at the same scale as the human figure.

1 **Megalodon** (extinct 2½ million years ago)
2 **whale shark**
3 **grizzly bear**
4 **African elephant**
5 **Moa** (extinct 1400 A.D.)
6 **oarfish**
7 **Argentinosaurus** (extinct 90 million years ago)
8 **hippopotamus**
9 **ground sloth** (extinct 6,250 years ago)
10 **blue whale**
11 **Titanboa** (extinct 58 million years ago)
12 **reticulated python**
13 **colossal squid**
14 **manta ray**
15 **Quetzalcoatlus** (extinct 66 million years ago)
16 **Mososaurus** (extinct 66 million years ago)
17 **saltwater crocodile**
18 **Sarcosuchus** (extinct 208 million years ago)
19 **Indricotherium** (extinct 23 million years ago)
20 **Tyrannoaurus rex** (extinct 66 million years ago)

Life size

These animals—some of the smallest of their kind—are shown at actual size.

1 bee hummingbird
2 dwarf goby
3 Amau frog
4 pygmy seahorse
5 *Brookseia* chameleon
6 *Wolfi* octopus
7 thread snake
8 bumblebee bat

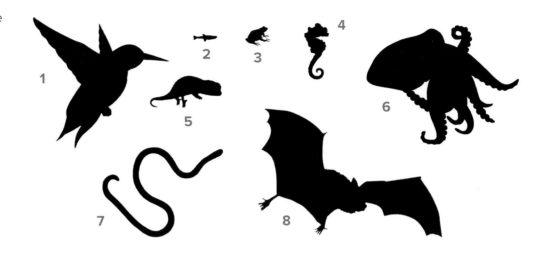

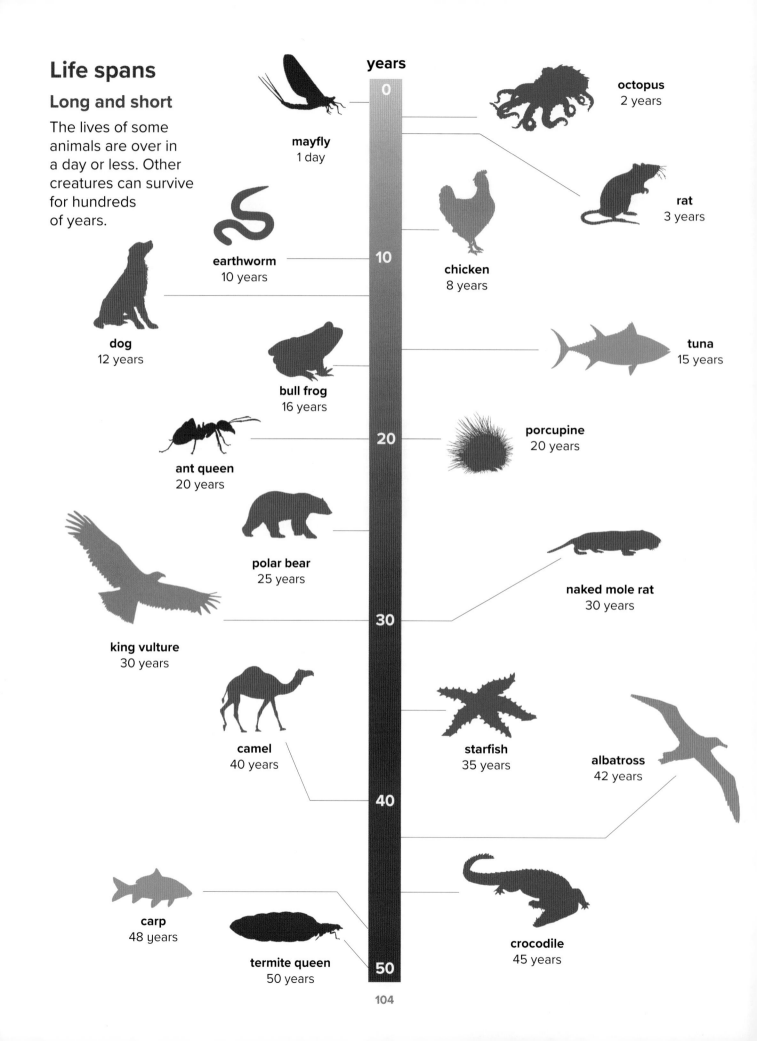

Life spans

Long and short

The lives of some animals are over in a day or less. Other creatures can survive for hundreds of years.

years

0

10

20

30

40

50

mayfly
1 day

octopus
2 years

rat
3 years

earthworm
10 years

chicken
8 years

dog
12 years

tuna
15 years

bull frog
16 years

ant queen
20 years

porcupine
20 years

polar bear
25 years

naked mole rat
30 years

king vulture
30 years

camel
40 years

starfish
35 years

albatross
42 years

carp
48 years

termite queen
50 years

crocodile
45 years

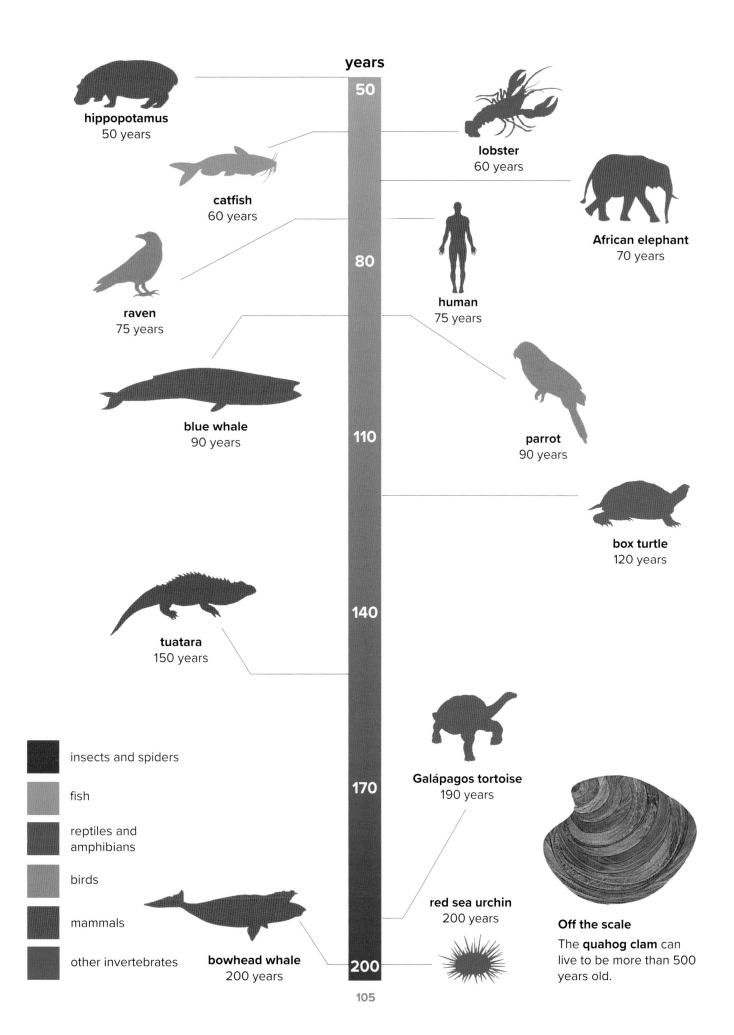

years

50

hippopotamus
50 years

lobster
60 years

catfish
60 years

African elephant
70 years

80

raven
75 years

human
75 years

blue whale
90 years

parrot
90 years

110

box turtle
120 years

140

tuatara
150 years

Galápagos tortoise
190 years

170

red sea urchin
200 years

Off the scale

The **quahog clam** can
live to be more than 500
years old.

bowhead whale
200 years

200

insects and spiders

fish

reptiles and
amphibians

birds

mammals

other invertebrates

Endangered animals

Almost gone

These animals are among the most endangered on Earth. There are fewer than 100 of any of these creatures still alive.

● = one animal

What is threatening them?

 habitat loss

collecting

hunting/poaching

fishing/poaching

The **Red River giant soft-shelled turtle** is perhaps the world's most endangered animal. As far as we know, there are just three of these turtles still alive. Two are in zoos, and one is in a lake in Vietnam.

Animal	Population	Threats
Miami blue butterfly fewer than 100 left	●●●●●●●●●●●●●●●●●●●●●●●●●●●●●●●●●●●● ●●●●●●●●●●●●●●●●●●●●●●●●●●●●●●●●●●●● ●●●●●●●●●●●●●●●●●●●●●●●●●●●●●●●●●●●● ●●●●●●●●●●●	habitat loss, collecting
Golden-headed langur 70 left	●●●●●●●●●●●●●●●●●●●●●●●●●●●●●●●●●●●● ●●●●●●●●●●●●●●●●●●●●●●●●●●●●●●●●●●●● ●●●●●●●●●●	habitat loss, hunting/poaching
Javan rhino 60 left	●●●●●●●●●●●●●●●●●●●●●●●●●●●●●● ●●●●●●●●●●●●●●●●●●●●●●●●●●●●●●●●	habitat loss, hunting/poaching
Spix macaw 40 left	●●●●●●●●●●●●●●●●●●●●●●●●●●●●●● ●●●●●●●●●●	habitat loss, collecting
Amur leopard 35 left	●●●●●●●●●●●●●●●●●●●●●●●●●●●●●● ●●●●●	habitat loss, hunting/poaching
Bajii dolphin 20 left (?)	●●●●●●●●●●●●●●●●●●●●	habitat loss, fishing/poaching
Red River soft-shelled turtle 3 left	●●●	habitat loss, fishing/poaching

The **bajii** is a freshwater dolphin native to China's Yangtze River. Its population of 20 is a guess—it may already be extinct.

The world's most endangered primate is the **golden-headed langur.** It is hunted for food and its forest home is being cut down.

In 1992, a hurricane destroyed the only known colony of the **Miami blue butterfly**. A few years later, another small colony of these rare insects was discovered in Florida.

Poachers kill the **Javan rhinoceros** because they mistakenly believe its horn has magical properties.

The **Amur leopard** is the world's most endangered large cat. It has been hunted almost to extinction for its fur.

A few years ago, only 17 **Spix macaws** were alive. Since then, birds bred in captivity have begun to increase their numbers.

Mass extinctions

Disaster!

Earth has experienced at least five mass extinctions within the past 500 million years. Each of these events caused more than half of the animal species alive at the time to become extinct. But these disasters also produced some winners: animals who were able to thrive once their competitors were gone.

In each mass extinction, many kinds of animals die off, leaving the field clear for other, luckier creatures. The graphs show only a few of the most well known.

Dinosaurs are probably the most famous extinct animals. But they are not alone—more than 99 percent of all the animals that have ever lived are now extinct. Many of them died out in one of the five great mass extinctions.

 percent of species that became extinct

 percent of species that survived

Possible causes of extinction

 climate change

 volcanic activity

 asteroid or comet impact

 human activity

500 million years ago   450 million years ago   400 million years ago   350 million years ago

440 million years ago

85% of animal species died

losers: nautiloids, corals, shellfish

winners: crinoids *(plantlike animals)*

The earth was colder, and glaciers locked up much of the world's water. No animals lived on land.

360 million years ago

75% of animal species died

losers: armored **fish**, corals

winners: sharks and bony fish

This event lasted around 20 million years. It could have been the result of drastic climate and sea level changes.

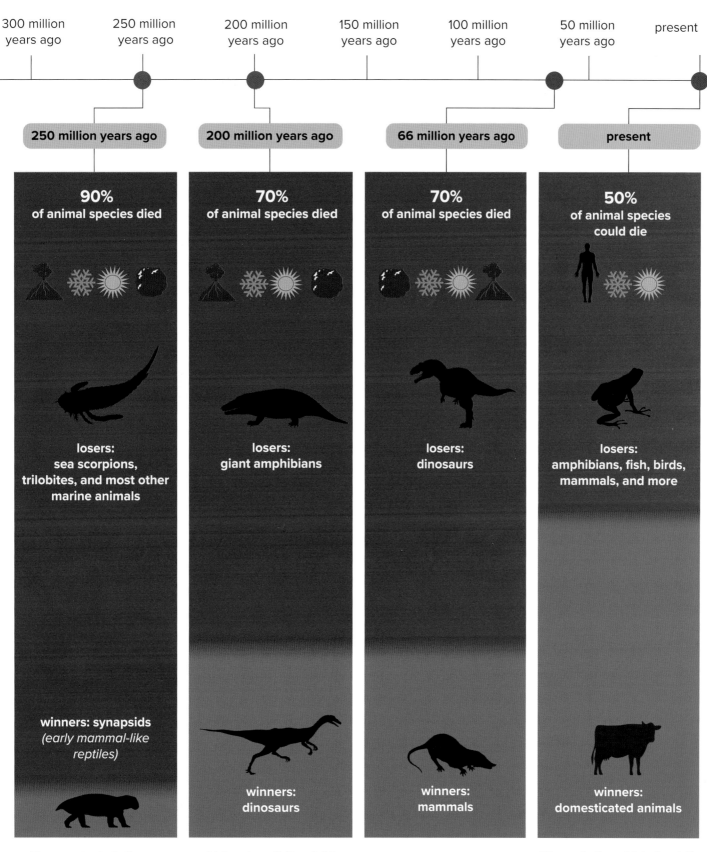

| 300 million years ago | 250 million years ago | 200 million years ago | 150 million years ago | 100 million years ago | 50 million years ago | present |

250 million years ago

90%
of animal species died

losers:
sea scorpions, trilobites, and most other marine animals

winners: synapsids
(early mammal-like reptiles)

The greatest of all mass extinctions. It may have been caused by an asteroid or comet impact, volcanic activity, or both.

200 million years ago

70%
of animal species died

losers:
giant amphibians

winners:
dinosaurs

Volcanic activity might be the main cause of this extinction.

66 million years ago

70%
of animal species died

losers:
dinosaurs

winners:
mammals

A city-size asteroid crashed into the Earth, causing terrible destruction. Massive lava flows probably contributed.

present

50%
of animal species could die

losers:
amphibians, fish, birds, mammals, and more

winners:
domesticated animals

We are in the midst of a sixth mass extinction caused by humans. In the next 50 years, half of all animal species could die.

More animals are extinct

The bad news: on average, an animal species becomes extinct after about 10 million years. The good news: modern humans have existed for only about 200,000 years.

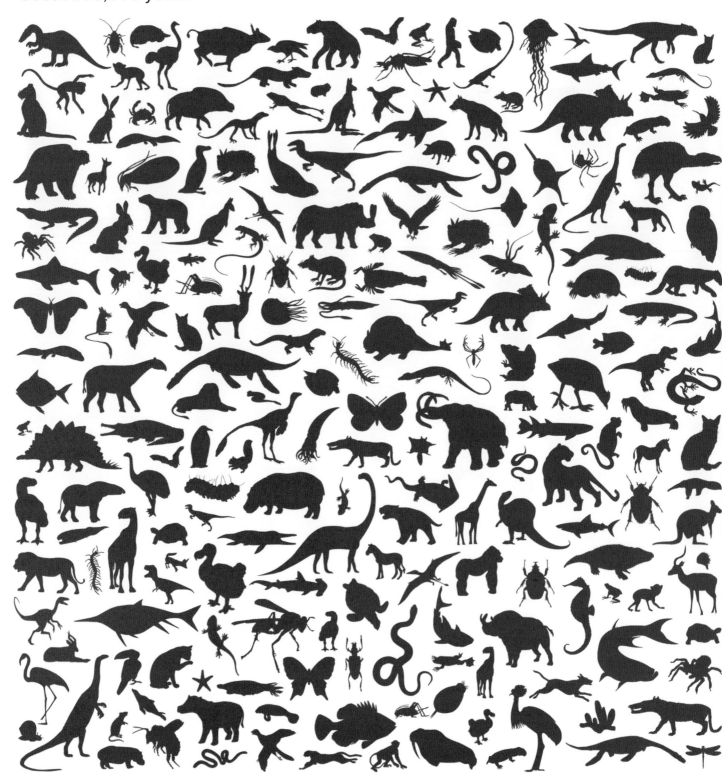

For every species alive
today, there are probably
1,000 that have died out,
or gone extinct.

Earth
Disasters caused by
movements of the Earth

Weather
Disasters caused by wind,
water, and extremes of
temperature

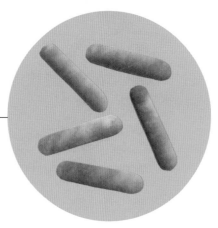

Life
Disasters caused by
living things

DISASTERS ON EARTH

The Earth is a restless planet. Continents collide in slow motion, causing earthquakes and volcanoes. Mountains rise and fall, and violent storms come and go. These things have been going on for billions of years. But when humans and their homes and towns and cities are affected by one of these events, the result is called a natural disaster. Some disasters, such as earthquakes, are sudden and unstoppable. Others, like droughts and sea level rise, happen in what seems to us like slow motion. Many of these events would happen whether people were here or not. Others are the result of something humans have done to the planet without understanding the consequences. Most natural disasters are local, affecting just one part of the Earth. But a few threaten the entire planet and everyone living on it.

* Words in blue can be found in the glossary on page 154.

Multiple effects • Natural disasters can be complicated

Most of the natural disasters looked at here can be organized into categories: **earth**, **weather**, and **life**. But many disasters have multiple effects. Some are immediate, while others are felt long after the original event. For example, a series of disastrous events often follows a large volcanic eruption.

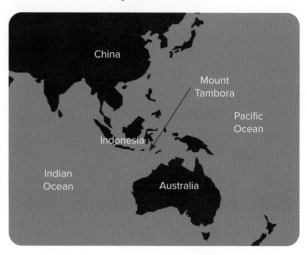

Tambora

In April of 1815, Mount Tambora, a volcano in Indonesia, exploded. It was the most powerful volcanic eruption of the past 10,000 years.

Pyroclastic flow

Superheated ash and gas flowed down the volcano at more than 100 mph (160 kph).*

Tsunami

The shock of the eruption created a tsunami—a giant wave.

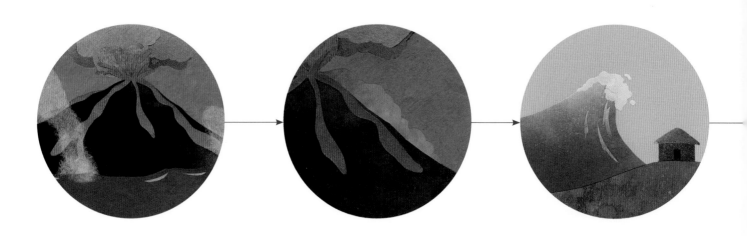

The force of the blast destroyed anything living within a few miles of the volcano.

The pyroclastic flow killed anything left alive on the island. More than 10,000 people were killed almost instantly.

The surge of water washed away towns and villages on nearby islands.

Timeline of a large explosive eruption and its aftereffects

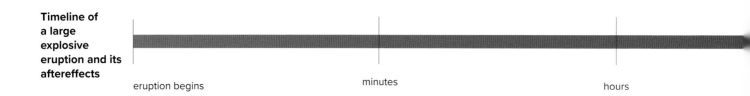

eruption begins

minutes

hours

*mph = miles per hour
kph = kilometers per hour

114

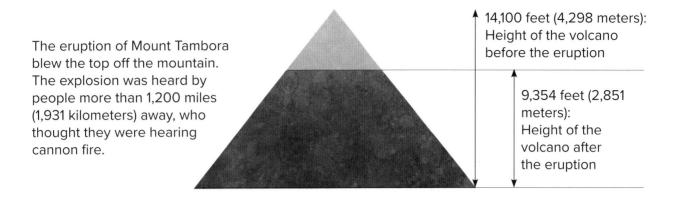

The eruption of Mount Tambora blew the top off the mountain. The explosion was heard by people more than 1,200 miles (1,931 kilometers) away, who thought they were hearing cannon fire.

14,100 feet (4,298 meters): Height of the volcano before the eruption

9,354 feet (2,851 meters): Height of the volcano after the eruption

Ash fall

Ash and pumice—volcanic rock—rained down over a huge area. In some places it was many feet deep.

Atmospheric effects

Gases from the volcano were blasted high into the atmosphere. They mixed with water to form tiny droplets of sulfuric acid.

Global cooling

Many parts of the world were unusually cold in 1816 and 1817.

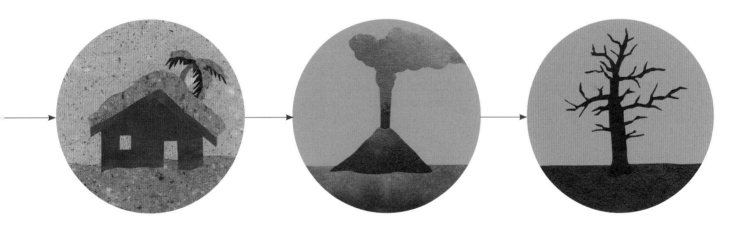

The weight of the ash collapsed houses and killed crops and livestock on the surrounding islands. As a result, 80,000 people perished of starvation and disease.

High-altitude winds spread the droplets around the world. They reflected sunlight back into space and cooled the planet.

In some places, the cold weather caused crops to fail and livestock to perish. Over the next year or two, thousands of people around the world died of starvation.

hours to weeks

weeks to months

months to years

Earthquakes • The Earth moves

Earth's crust is broken into more than a dozen pieces, called tectonic plates. The plates—and the continents on them—are in constant motion. On average, they move at about the same speed that your fingernails grow. Most earthquakes occur where two plates meet. As they slide past each other, the plates can get stuck, sometimes for centuries. Pressure builds up until the plates suddenly move, releasing energy and shaking the ground.

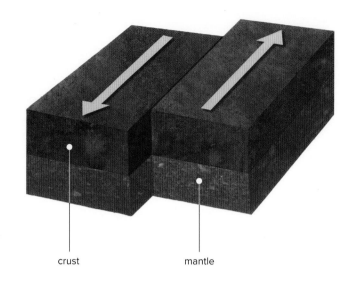

crust   mantle

Deadly earthquakes

There are hundreds of thousands of earthquakes every year. Most can only be detected by scientific instruments, but about 100 each year are strong enough to cause damage. The graph below highlights a few of the serious quakes of the past 500 years.

The size of the circles on the graph represents the number of fatalities caused by each earthquake.

Shaanxi, China

1556
The deadliest earthquake in recorded history

Sicily, Italy

1693

Lisbon, Portugal

1755

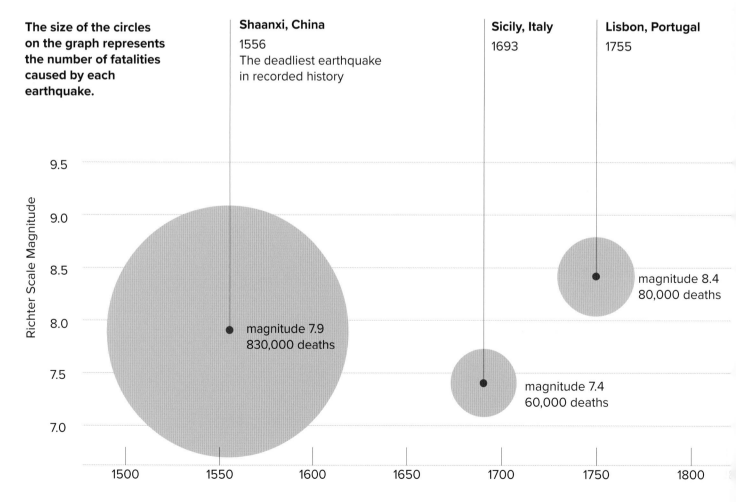

magnitude 7.9
830,000 deaths

magnitude 8.4
80,000 deaths

magnitude 7.4
60,000 deaths

Richter Scale Magnitude

Some of the things that make an earthquake deadly

 Building collapse, falling masonry

 Fire (caused by broken gas lines or overturned oil lamps)

 Tsunami

 Liquefaction—intense vibration makes wet soil act like a liquid

 Landslide or avalanche

The Richter Scale

There are different ways of measuring the strength of an earthquake. One of the most commonly used is the Richter Scale, which ranks earthquakes on a 1–9 scale. Each step on the scale represents a 10X increase in magnitude (a magnitude 4 quake is ten times as powerful as a magnitude 3 quake).

1 Usually not felt.

2 Some people feel movement. Hanging fixtures sway slightly.

3 Most people notice. Objects indoors may shake or rattle.

4 Noticeable shaking. Objects may fall off shelves. Slight damage to structures.

5 Furniture may fall over. Major damage to poorly built structures.

6 Moderate to severe damage to most buildings. Difficult to remain standing.

7 Almost all structures damaged. Many buildings collapse. Impossible to remain standing.

8 Most buildings severely damaged or destroyed. People and objects thrown into the air.

9 The surface of the earth buckles. Total destruction of almost all buildings.

Arica, Chile
1868

San Francisco, United States
1906

Valdivia, Chile
1960
The most powerful earthquake ever recorded

Tangshan, China
1976

Banda Aceh, Indonesia
2004

9.5

magnitude 9.2
225,000 deaths

9.0

magnitude 9.5
25,000 deaths

magnitude 9.0
25,000 deaths

8.5

magnitude 7.9
3,000 deaths

8.0

magnitude 7.6
240,000 deaths

7.5

7.0

350   1900   1950   2000

Volcanoes • Lava, ash, and fire

The crust of the Earth is a layer of rock about as thick, compared to the Earth as a whole, as an apple's skin is to an apple. The crust floats on the mantle, a much thicker layer of hot rock that contains pockets of molten rock, or magma. Sometimes magma reaches the surface and escapes in a volcanic eruption. Some of these eruptions are gentle. Others are powerfully explosive.

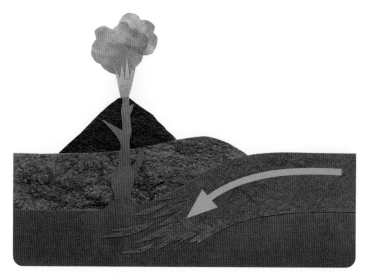

Many volcanoes occur where two crustal plates meet. One section of crust dives beneath another and is melted by the heat of the mantle. The molten rock, or magma, rises and bursts from the surface as a volcano.

Volcanic dangers

What makes a volcano deadly?

Ash cloud

Ash can choke people and collapse buildings. When blasted high into the atmosphere, ash blocks sunlight. In a large eruption, this can cool the entire planet and eventually cause crops to fail and people to starve.

Explosive blast

A violent eruption can be as powerful as a nuclear bomb.

Mud and water

Snow and ice melt and rush down the volcano, carrying ash and dirt. These mudflows are called *lahars*.

Tsunami

If the volcano is near the sea, the eruption can create giant waves—a tsunami.

Volcanic bombs

Chunks of rock and lava as big as a car can be hurled for miles.

Pyroclastic flow

A cloud of red-hot dust and ash moves at high speed and kills any living thing it touches.

Lava flow

Molten rock burns everything in its path.

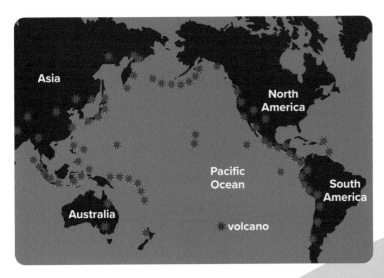

Three-quarters of Earth's volcanoes are found on the **Ring of Fire**, a chain of volcanoes around the Pacific Ocean. They occur where the Pacific Plate collides with other tectonic plates.

VEI 5
Mount St. Helens
Washington,
United States, 1980
57 deaths

VEI 6
Santa María
Guatemala, 1902
5,000 deaths

VEI 6
Novarupta
Alaska,
United States, 1912
no deaths
(The eruption
occurred in an
uninhabited area.)

VEI 6
Krakatoa
Indonesia, 1883
36,000 deaths

The VEI

Volcanoes are rated from 1 to 8 on the VEI (Volcanic Explosivity Index). This scale is based on the force of the eruption and on the amount of lava, ash, and rock ejected. An eruption that can cause serious local damage occurs somewhere on Earth about once every 10 years. Eruptions that seriously affect the entire planet are much rarer, taking place about once every 10,000 years.

VEI 7
Tambora
Indonesia, 1815
90,000 deaths

This is the largest eruption of the past 10,000 years, and the eruption with the greatest human death toll.

VEI 8
Toba
Sumatra
75,000 years ago
deaths unknown

This is the largest eruption of the past 25 million years. It ejected enough ash, rocks, and lava to cover a thousand football fields to a depth of two miles (3.2 kilometers).

VEI 8
Taupō
New Zealand
26,000 years ago
deaths unknown

The size of the circles represents the amount of material ejected in an eruption.

Tsunamis • Get to high ground!

In the open ocean, a tsunami—an unusually large wave or set of waves—travels at speeds of up to 500 mph (805 kph). But when the tsunami waves reach shallow water, they slow down and grow taller, sometimes reaching heights of 100 feet (30 meters) or more. Depending upon where the tsunami originated, people in low-lying coastal areas have anywhere from a few minutes to a few hours to get away from the coast or climb to safety.

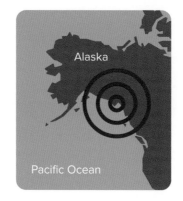

The largest tsunami ever witnessed occurred in Alaska in 1958. An earthquake dropped millions of tons of rock into Lituya Bay. The resulting wave was 1,720 feet (524 meters) high.

The deadliest tsunami in history occurred in Indonesia in 2004. An undersea earthquake created waves that killed more than 225,000 people.

time elapsed: seconds   5 minutes

Most tsunamis are caused by earthquakes

Timeline of a large tsunami ⟶ A powerful quake takes place beneath the seafloor.

The spreading water forms a series of fast-moving waves. In deep water, they are only a foot or two high and often go unnoticed.

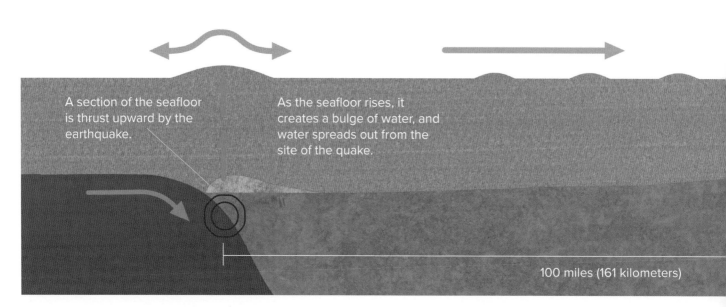

A section of the seafloor is thrust upward by the earthquake.

As the seafloor rises, it creates a bulge of water, and water spreads out from the site of the quake.

100 miles (161 kilometers)

Tsunamis can also be caused by

Explosive **volcanic eruptions**

Landslides, which are sometimes the result of an erupting volcano or an earthquake. An underwater landslide can also create a tsunami.

Meteorites and **asteroids** hitting the water. These events are rare, but can be devastating.

Large chunks of **ice** breaking off a glacier and falling into the sea

12 minutes

15 minutes

As the waves reach shallower water, they begin to slow and build in height.

Eventually, the waves break and wash over low-lying coasts. In some tsunamis, waves a few minutes apart can continue to arrive for hours.

Sometimes tsunami waves don't curl and break, but act more like a fast-moving high tide. This is why tsunamis are sometimes called "tidal waves," even though they don't have any connection to the tides (which are caused by the gravitational pull of the Moon and Sun).

Landslides • Dirt, rocks, and mud

Mountains are constantly being eroded—worn down by wind and rain. This is usually a gradual process that happens over millions of years. But sometimes mountainsides come crashing down in the blink of an eye.

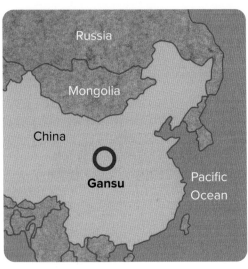

In 2010, heavy rains fell on Gansu, China. In some areas, it rained four inches (10 centimeters) in one hour. A wall of rocks and mud five stories high swept down a river and through several towns, killing more than 1,700 people.

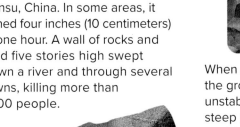

What causes landslides and mudslides?

Heavy rainfall softens and weakens the soil that holds hillsides in place.

One of the effects of a **volcanic eruption** can be a lahar—a surge of mud and ash carried by melted snow and ice.

When an **earthquake** shakes the ground, it can cause unstable rocks and soil on steep mountainsides to tumble downhill.

When a **wildfire** destroys the vegetation that helps hold a hillside in place, even a light rain can cause mud and rocks to tumble downhill.

Avalanches • Snow and ice

Snow can accumulate on steep mountain slopes until something disturbs it. When that happens, a mass of snow and ice can break loose and slide downhill at speeds of more than 200 mph (322 kph). It's an avalanche, and it can snap big trees like matchsticks and bury a skier—or a whole town.

Most avalanches are caused by people—skiers, hikers, or snowmobilers. Slides typically happen on slopes between 30 and 50 degrees.

fracture zone—where the avalanche starts

a sliding mass of snow and ice

runout zone—where most victims are buried

The deadliest avalanche

In 1970, a magnitude 7.9 earthquake struck off the coast of Peru. The quake shook loose the deadliest avalanche ever recorded. More than 20,000 people were killed.

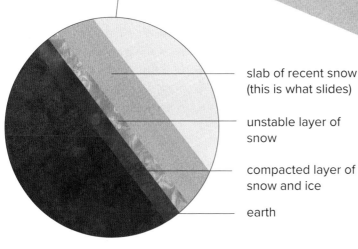

slab of recent snow (this is what slides)

unstable layer of snow

compacted layer of snow and ice

earth

A single snowflake is delicate and almost weightless. But when enough snowflakes pile up and start to slide, the results can be disastrous.

Hurricanes • Killer storms

In different parts of the world, intense tropical storms are called hurricanes, typhoons, or cyclones. They are the most powerful storms on Earth, and they can last for days, with destructive winds, deadly storm surge, and heavy rainfall.

How storms are named

Every tropical storm is given a name, alternating between male and female names. Different parts of the world use different lists of names. For storms in the Atlantic, the names begin with the letter *A* and proceed in alphabetical order. The names for 2022 begin with Alex, Bonnie, Colin, and Danielle.

If there are more than twenty-one named storms in the Atlantic (the letters *Q, U, X, Y,* and *Z* are not used), there is a second set of male and female names that will be used.

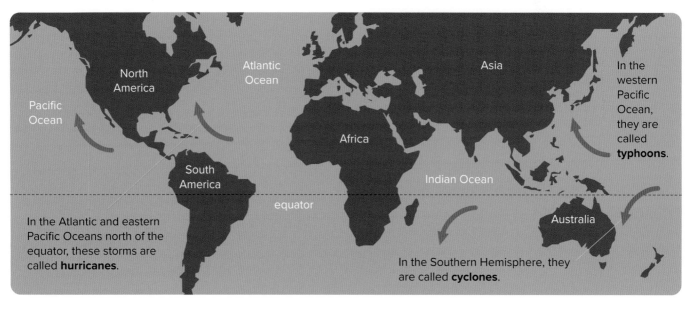

In the western Pacific Ocean, they are called **typhoons**.

In the Atlantic and eastern Pacific Oceans north of the equator, these storms are called **hurricanes**.

In the Southern Hemisphere, they are called **cyclones**.

Anatomy of a hurricane

average width of storm = 300 miles (483 kilometers)

average width of eye = 30 miles (48 kilometers)

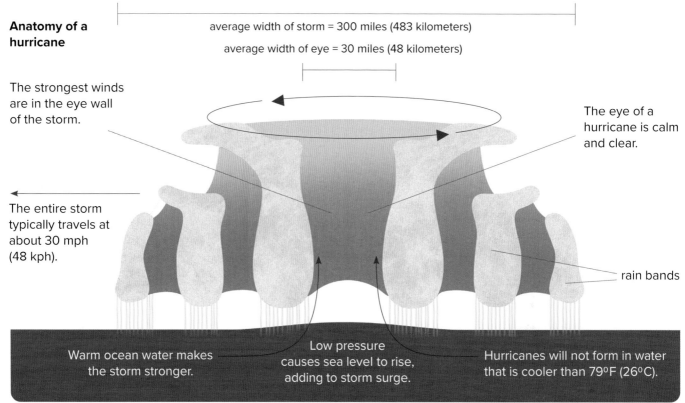

The strongest winds are in the eye wall of the storm.

The eye of a hurricane is calm and clear.

The entire storm typically travels at about 30 mph (48 kph).

rain bands

Warm ocean water makes the storm stronger.

Low pressure causes sea level to rise, adding to storm surge.

Hurricanes will not form in water that is cooler than 79°F (26°C).

Due to the rotation of the earth, tropical storms rotate counterclockwise in the Northern Hemisphere . . .

. . . and clockwise in the Southern Hemisphere.

Record wind speeds

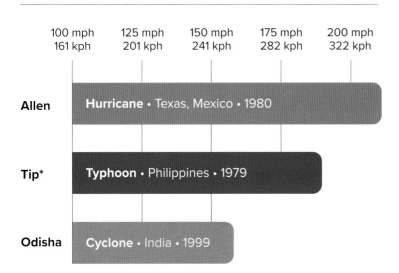

100 mph 161 kph	125 mph 201 kph	150 mph 241 kph	175 mph 282 kph	200 mph 322 kph

Allen — Hurricane • Texas, Mexico • 1980

Tip* — Typhoon • Philippines • 1979

Odisha — Cyclone • India • 1999

* 1,380 miles (2,221 km.) in diameter—largest tropical storm ever measured

The hurricane intensity scale is based on wind speed

Category 1
75–95 mph (121–153 kph) winds

Some broken tree branches, damage to house roofs and powerlines.

Category 2
96–110 mph (154–177 kph) winds

Some trees uprooted. Serious damage to homes and other structures. Some roofs blown off.

Category 3
111–129 mph (178–208 kph) winds

Extensive damage to homes and commercial buildings. Many trees toppled. Loss of electricity and running water for days or weeks.

Category 4
130–156 mph (209–251 kph) winds

Catastrophic damage to houses and other structures. Many destroyed. Roads impassable due to flooding and downed trees. Power and water supply lost for weeks or months.

Category 5
higher than 157 mph (252 kph) winds

Almost complete destruction of houses and buildings. Deadly storm surge. Area left uninhabitable for weeks or months.

Tornadoes • Twister!

A tornado forms when some of the energy in a thunderstorm is converted into a spinning column of air that reaches from the clouds to the ground. Tornadoes are much smaller than hurricanes, but wind speeds in a tornado can be higher. Tornadoes can cause massive damage to buildings, vehicles, livestock, and people.

Tornadoes occur in many parts of the world.

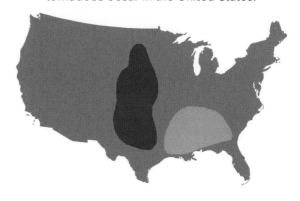

But more than four out of five of the world's tornadoes occur in the United States.

 Where tornadoes happen	In 1989, the deadliest tornado in history killed 1,300 people in Bangladesh.	Two areas in the American Midwest and South are known for frequent and violent tornadoes.	Tornado Alley / Dixie Alley

---

Taking a tornado ride

People caught in a tornado may be killed or injured by flying debris or by being dropped from a great height. But a few people have been sucked into the air, spun around, and set back down without much damage. These three lucky people (and one pony) survived their encounter with a tornado with only minor scrapes.

Tennessee, 2008
An eleven-month-old baby was torn from his mother's arms, lifted into the air, and set down 300 feet (91 meters) away.

South Dakota, 1955
A nine-year-old girl and her pony were picked up and carried 1,000 feet (305 meters).

Missouri, 2006
A nineteen-year-old man was sucked out of a trailer and carried 1,307 feet (398 meters).

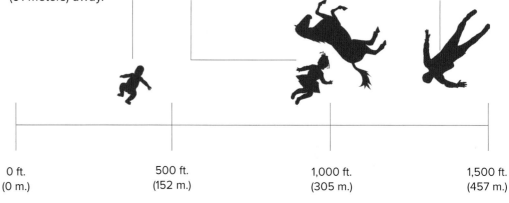

0 ft. (0 m.)	500 ft. (152 m.)	1,000 ft. (305 m.)	1,500 ft. (457 m.)

The tornado rating scale

Tornadoes are rated on a five-step scale called the EF Scale. It is based on maximum wind speeds and the amount of damage done by a tornado on the ground.

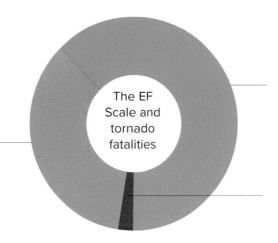

The EF Scale and tornado fatalities

Sixty-five percent of tornadoes are rated **EF-0** or **EF-1**. These twisters cause few deaths.

Thirty-three percent of tornadoes are rated **EF-2** or **EF-3**. They cause 30 percent of tornado-related deaths.

Only 2 percent of tornadoes are rated **EF-4** or **EF-5**, but they cause 70 percent of tornado-related deaths.

Weak: EF-0 and EF-1

65–110 mph
(105–177 kph) winds

Slight to moderate damage to trees and buildings

Strong: EF-2 and EF-3

111–165 mph
(179–266 kph) winds

Serious damage to trees and buildings
Extensive power outages

Devastating: EF-4 and EF-5

166–over 200 mph
(267–over 322 kph) winds

Total destruction of most structures
Cars and trucks flipped and blown away

Tornado records

The Tri-State Tornado of 1925 holds multiple tornado records. It stayed on the ground for 3½ hours (most tornadoes last for just a few minutes). It also holds the record for fastest-moving tornado—at one point, it was clocked at 73 mph (117 kph). Its path was 219 miles (352 kilometers) long, and it killed 695 people—making it the second most deadly tornado in history.

The El Reno, Oklahoma, EF-3 tornado of 2013 was the widest tornado ever measured.

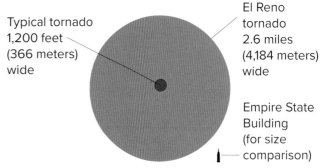

Typical tornado 1,200 feet (366 meters) wide

El Reno tornado 2.6 miles (4,184 meters) wide

Empire State Building (for size comparison)

The highest wind speed ever observed on Earth was in the Bridge Creek–Moore EF-5 tornado of 1999 in Oklahoma.

65 mph (105 kph)	EF-0 (minimum wind speed)
200 mph (322 kph)	EF-5 (minimum wind speed)
318 mph (512 kph)	Bridge Creek–Moore wind speed

0 mph (0 kph)   90 mph (145 kph)   180 mph (290 kph)   270 mph (435 kph)   360 mph (579 kph)

Path of the Tri-State Tornado through the American Midwest

Floods · Rising water

In some floods, the water is calm and rises slowly. But in a *flash flood,* a turbulent, fast-moving wall of water arrives without warning. Floods may be the result of heavy rains, storm-driven surges, or the collapse of natural or man-made dams.

storm winds push water onshore

15-foot storm surge

normal high tide line

sea level

Storm surge
In 1900, a hurricane came ashore at Galveston, Texas. It brought a 15-foot (4½-meter) storm surge and caused 8,000 deaths, most of them by drowning.

1

2

3

Quake, slide, flood
In 1841, in what is now Pakistan, (**1**) an earthquake triggered a landslide that blocked the Indus River for months. (**2**) A 500-foot-deep (152-meter-deep) lake formed. (**3**) When the natural rock dam failed, it released what was probably the largest flood in recorded history. No one knows how many people were killed, but it must have been many thousands.

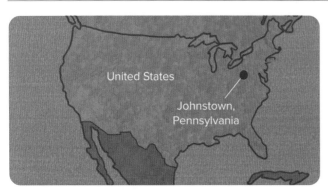

United States

Johnstown, Pennsylvania

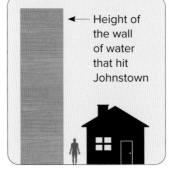

Height of the wall of water that hit Johnstown

Dam failure
The dam above Johnstown, Pennsylvania, was man-made. But days of heavy rain caused it to collapse in 1889. It was the deadliest flash flood in US history. More than 2,200 people were killed when a 40-foot (12-meter) wall of water swept through the town.

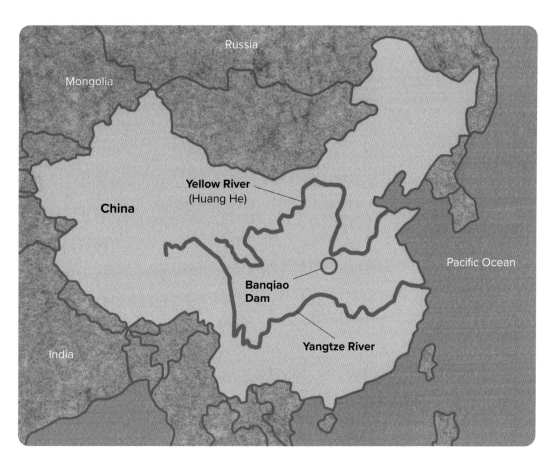

The China floods

China has experienced more deadly floods than any other country. The Yangtze River—the third-longest river in the world—has repeatedly overflowed its banks. The Yellow River, or Huang He, has also flooded many times. These rivers run through low, fertile lands that are home to millions of people.

1887

Yellow River flood

After heavy rains, the river overflowed a system of dikes.

900,000 fatalities

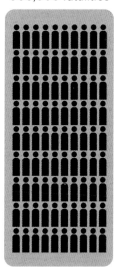

1931

Yangtze River floods

One of the worst natural disasters of all time. The flooding, due to heavy rains, lasted for several months.

2,000,000 fatalities

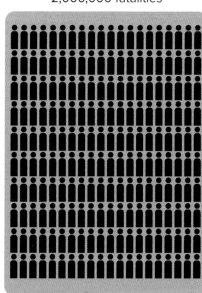

1935

Yangtze River flood

Caused by unusually heavy rainfall

145,000 fatalities

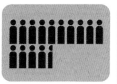

1938

Yellow River flood

China was at war. Dikes were intentionally breached to slow the Japanese army.

500,000 fatalities

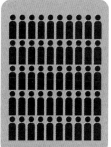

1975

Banqiao Dam

This dam, on the Ru River in central China, failed after intense rains.

230,000 fatalities

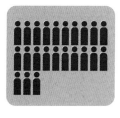

Each figure represents 10,000 deaths.

Thunderstorms • Wind, rain, lightning, and hail

Severe thunderstorms can be deadly. The heavy rain that often accompanies a storm can cause flash floods. Wind and hail can damage property and sometimes injure or even kill people. Tornadoes get their start in thunderstorms. And lightning kills thousands of people a year.

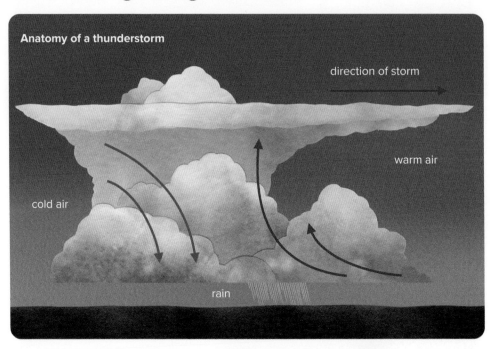

Anatomy of a thunderstorm

direction of storm

warm air

cold air

rain

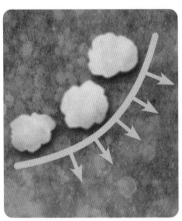

Thunderstorms often take on the shape of an anvil. The technical name of a thunderstorm cloud is cumulonimbus, but it is often called an anvil cloud. ▶

◀ Sometimes a line of thunderstorms creates a band of hurricane-force winds that can be hundreds of miles wide. This dangerous phenomenon is called a *derecho* (*de-**ray**-cho*).

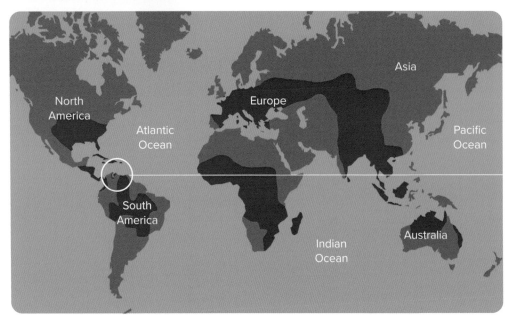

North America

Atlantic Ocean

South America

Europe

Asia

Pacific Ocean

Indian Ocean

Australia

Thunderstorm hot spots
The areas in red experience at least 20 thunderstorms a year. At any given time, there are about 2,000 thunderstorms happening around the world.

The top thunderstorm and lightning spot in the world is a lake in Venezuela, where there is, on average, a thunderstorm 300 days a year.

Shocking

Lightning always accompanies a thunderstorm, and is the cause of many deaths, injuries, and forest fires.

Ice from the sky

Hail—solid balls of ice that can be as small as a blueberry or as large as a cantaloupe—sometimes falls during a thunderstorm. Large hail can damage cars, buildings, trees, and crops. It can even be deadly. A hailstorm in India in 1888 killed more than 230 people.

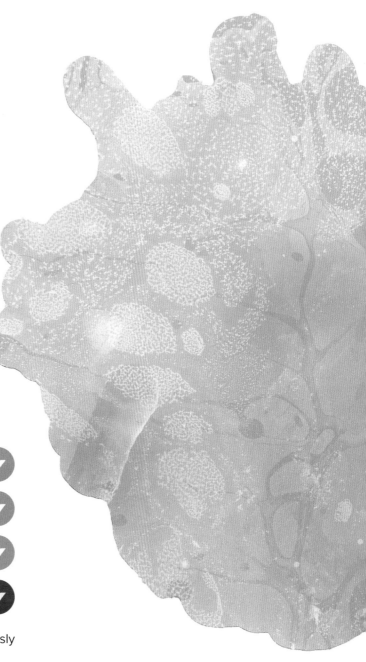

Lightning casualties

Each symbol represents 6,000 people. About 240,000 people a year are struck by lightning around the world. Serious injury results for about 180,000 of these victims. As many as 24,000 are killed.

 struck but not seriously injured

 seriously injured but not killed

 killed

Record hail

The largest hailstone ever measured fell in South Dakota in 2010. It was eight inches (20 centimeters) in diameter. (Shown here at actual size)

Blizzards • Snow and wind

There are snowstorms, and then there are blizzards. A blizzard can bring a large area—even a big city—to a standstill. A blizzard's cold, wind, and snow combine to create potentially deadly conditions.

In January of 1888, a sudden drop in temperature and heavy, drifting snow caught people—and trains—unaware. The storm was called the Schoolhouse Blizzard, and it killed 235 people in the American Midwest.

What is a blizzard?

A snowstorm has to meet three requirements to be considered a blizzard:

❶ Wind

In a blizzard, the wind blows at least 35 mph (56 kph). In a severe blizzard, the wind blows at more than 45 mph (72 kph).

❷ Visibility

Blowing snow reduces visibility—the distance one can see before everything disappears in the snow—to less than ¼ mile (402 meters).

❸ Duration

The snowy, windy conditions must last for at least three hours.

`03:00`

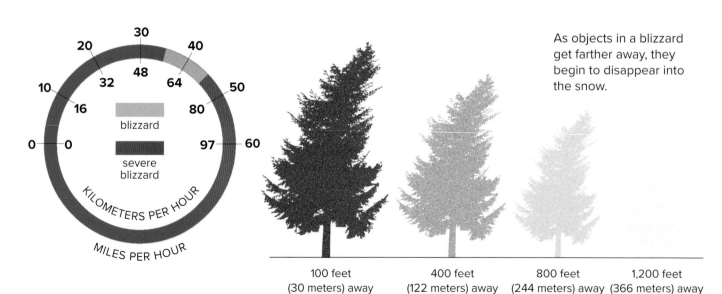

As objects in a blizzard get farther away, they begin to disappear into the snow.

100 feet (30 meters) away

400 feet (122 meters) away

800 feet (244 meters) away

1,200 feet (366 meters) away

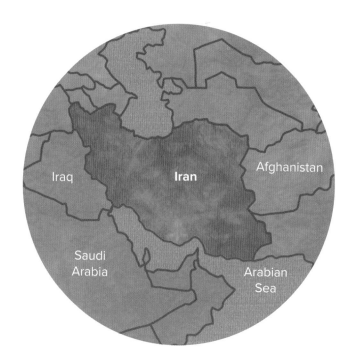

A deadly blizzard

Twenty-six feet (8 meters) of snow fell in Iran in a 1972 blizzard. Hundreds of villages were completely buried, and 4,000 people died.

26 feet (8 meters) of snow

The Great Blizzard of 1888

Fifty inches (1¼ meters) of snow fell on parts of New England. High winds created snowdrifts that were 50 feet (15 meters) deep in places, and 400 people died in the storm.

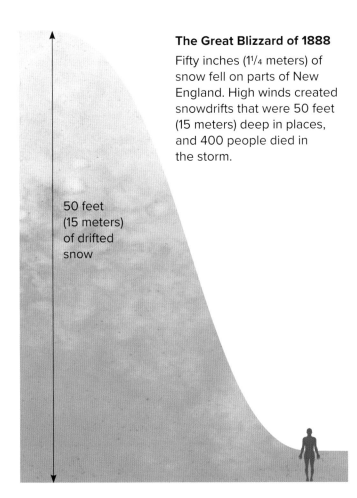

50 feet (15 meters) of drifted snow

What do volcanoes have to do with blizzards?

In 1883, the South Pacific island of Krakatoa exploded. It was one of the most powerful volcanic eruptions in recorded history. The ash and gases blasted into the atmosphere reflected sunlight and cooled the planet for several years. Scientists think that the eruption may have helped cause the intense blizzards of 1885–1888 in the United States.

Drought • Waiting for rain

A drought is a period of months or years in which there is less rainfall or snowfall than usual. This reduces moisture in the soil, lowers groundwater levels, and dries up lakes and streams. Aside from pandemics, droughts have been responsible for more human deaths than any other kind of natural disaster.

Ancient droughts

By looking at the growth rings in old trees and the sediments from long-ago lakes and rivers, scientists can tell when and where severe droughts occurred.

A moving wall of dirt

During a drought, the soil dries out and can be picked up and carried by the wind. It's a dust storm, and it can smother fields and fill houses with dirt. The midwestern United States endured repeated dust storms during the Dust Bowl of the 1930s.

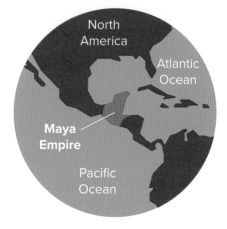

Out of Africa

Between 90,000 and 130,000 years ago, parts of Africa experienced a series of severe droughts. Lakes and rivers dried up, and forests turned to deserts. These changes may have given early humans a reason to leave Africa and spread into other parts of the world.

Egypt's Old Kingdom

Ancient Egypt was home to one of the most advanced civilizations in the world. But by 4,000 years ago, Egypt's Old Kingdom was in decline. There is evidence of a drought at the same time, which many historians believe led to the end of Egypt as a world power.

The Maya Empire

For hundreds of years, the Mayans of Central America built impressive temples and practiced advanced mathematics and astronomy. But about 1,200 years ago, the Maya Empire collapsed. One of the main reasons for their downfall might have been a series of droughts that lasted for decades.

Drought: cause and effects

low levels of rain- and snowfall

soil dries out

water level falls in lakes and rivers

groundwater is depleted

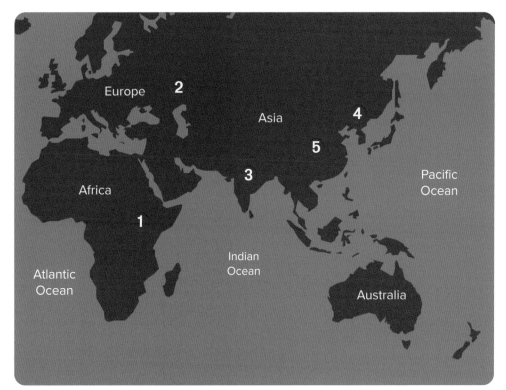

Drought and famine

Starvation is the most common cause of human death in a drought. When many people die from lack of food, it's called a famine. People weakened by lack of food are also more likely to die from disease. And droughts have led to war as people battled over limited supplies of water.

The map shows where some of the world's deadliest droughts have occurred.

❶ Ethiopian famine
1984–1985

The effects of a drought were made worse by war, which prevented aid from reaching starving people. More than one million people perished.

❷ Russian famine
1921–1922

Once again, crop failures caused by a drought were intensified by conflict and a political crisis. There were five million deaths.

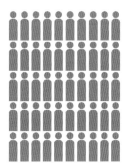

❸ Southern India famine
1876–1878

A widespread, severe drought affected much of Asia. In India, five and a half million people starved to death.

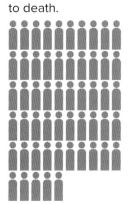

❹ North Korean famine
1994–1998

A drought—combined with the government's destructive policies—cost as many as two million lives.

❺ North China famine
1876–1879

The worst drought in China's history killed an estimated 11 million people.

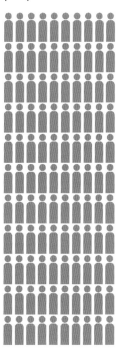

Each figure represents 100,000 human deaths.

Climate change and drought

The world is getting warmer at a rapid rate. As the climate warms, some parts of the world will get more rain and snow. But other parts will get much less. Higher temperatures are also drying out the soil more quickly.

See pages 146–147 for more information about climate change.

Extreme temperatures • Too hot!

Extreme heat and drought often go together. But droughts happen over months or years. Heat waves are spikes in the temperature that last for days or weeks. Heat waves can be deadly, especially for older people or people in poor health who don't have air-conditioning. The world is experiencing hotter and more frequent heat waves as the planet gets warmer.

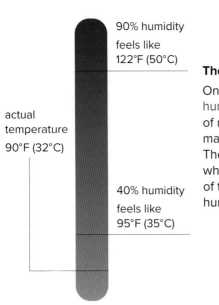

90% humidity feels like 122°F (50°C)

actual temperature 90°F (32°C)

40% humidity feels like 95°F (35°C)

The heat index

On hot days, high humidity—the amount of moisture in the air—makes it feel hotter. The heat index shows what a combination of temperature and humidity feels like.

What makes a heat wave deadly?

When it's very hot and there's no way to cool off, people are at risk for heatstroke. Normal body temperature is 98.6°F (37°C). But someone suffering from heatstroke will have a temperature of 104°F (40°C) or higher. Here are some of the other symptoms:

- Confusion
- Headache
- Nausea and vomiting
- Hot, dry skin. People with heatstroke don't sweat even though their body is overheated.
- Rapid heart rate

Heatstroke is a serious medical condition. The best way to treat it is by cooling off the person with an ice bath, cold water, or wet towels.

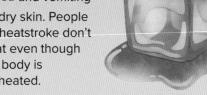

Some serious heat

A heat wave is five or more days in a row when the temperature is more than 9°F (5°C) warmer than the average high temperature.

Each figure represents 500 deaths from heat.

maximum temperature reached during a heat wave

Pakistan, 2015
Temperatures reached 120°F (49°C). Two thousand people died as a result of the heat.

Eastern United States, 1901
It reached 108°F (42¼°C). Six weeks of record-breaking heat left 9,500 dead.

Greece, 1967
One thousand people were killed by temperatures reaching 107°F (41½°C).

Chicago, United States, 1995
More than 700 people died as the temperature climbed to 106°F (41°C).

France, 2003
More than 14,000 people were killed by a heat wave in Europe that reached 104°F (40°C). Thousands more died in other European countries.

Argentina, 1900
Unusually high humidity and 99°F (37°C) temperatures left more than 400 people dead.

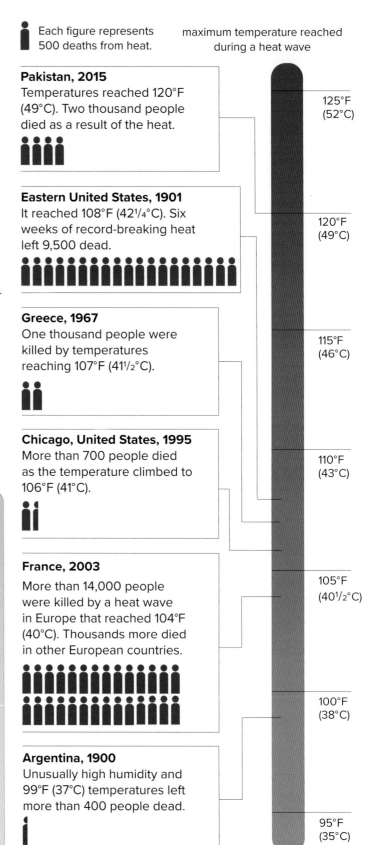

125°F (52°C)

120°F (49°C)

115°F (46°C)

110°F (43°C)

105°F (40½°C)

100°F (38°C)

95°F (35°C)

Extreme temperatures • Too cold!

A cold wave, also called a cold snap, happens when the temperature drops far below normal lows in a short period of time. Cold waves can be dangerous to humans and animals. They can freeze water supplies and cause power failures, which leaves many people without heat.

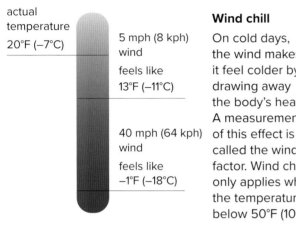

actual temperature
20°F (−7°C)

5 mph (8 kph) wind
feels like 13°F (−11°C)

40 mph (64 kph) wind
feels like −1°F (−18°C)

Wind chill
On cold days, the wind makes it feel colder by drawing away the body's heat. A measurement of this effect is called the wind chill factor. Wind chill only applies when the temperature is below 50°F (10°C).

What makes a cold wave dangerous?

The most serious danger to people in cold weather is hypothermia, when the body temperature falls below 95°F (35°C). It's critical to get help for someone with hypothermia or they can die. Here are some of the symptoms:

- Shivering
- Slurred speech
- Sleepiness
- Disorientation
- Fast heart rate

When someone has hypothermia, it's important to get medical help quickly. If that's not possible, the person should be warmed with dry clothing and blankets. Someone who is not cold can help by wrapping themselves up in a blanket along with the person experiencing hypothermia.

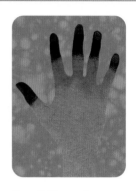

Frostbite—when exposed skin freezes and dies—is another risk of cold weather.

Some record cold temperatures around the world

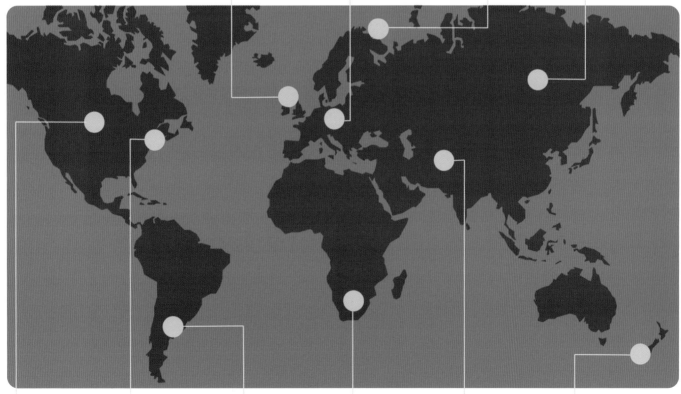

−15°F (−26°C)
England, 1982

−42°F (−41°C)
Czech Republic, 1929

−39°F (−39°C)
Finland, 2012

−48°F (−44°C)
Mongolia, 2010

−49°F (−45°C)
Montana, United States, 1899

−15°F (−26°C)
New York City, United States, 1934

−27°F (−33°C)
Argentina, 1907

−4°F (−20°C)
South Africa, 2013

−62°F (−52°C)
Afghanistan, 1964

−14°F (−26°C)
New Zealand, 1903

Fire • Increasing risk

As the climate warms, forests and grasslands dry out more quickly. This makes them vulnerable to wildfires. Sometimes the fires are started by a careless human tossing a cigarette into the grass. Other fires are started by downed power lines or lightning. However they begin, wildfires are one of nature's most terrifying spectacles. And once they start, they can spread quickly and burn forests, fields, and houses.

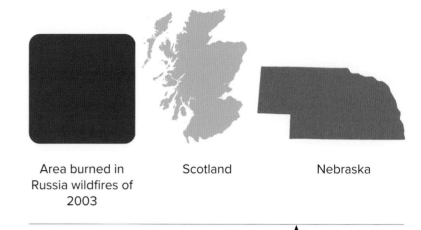

Area burned in Russia wildfires of 2003

Scotland

Nebraska

The area burned by a few historical wildfires

Russia: wildfires 2003
burned 77,000 square miles (200,000 square kilometers)

An area about the size of Scotland or the state of Nebraska. These were the largest wildfires ever recorded.

fatalities unknown

Australia: Black Summer 2019–2020
burned 73,000 square miles (189,000 square kilometers)

450 deaths

China: Black Dragon Fire 1987
burned 28,000 square miles (73,000 square kilometers)

200 deaths

Canada: Manitoba fires 1989
burned 12,664 square miles (33,000 square kilometers)

no reported fatalities

United States: West Coast 2020
burned 9,188 square miles (24,000 square kilometers) in California, Oregon, and Washington

40 deaths

Michigan: Peshtigo Fire 1871
burned 1,875 square miles (4,600 square kilometers)

1,200 to 2,500 deaths—the most caused by any wildfire in America

Fighting fires

Earthquakes, tornadoes, and many other natural disasters happen without warning, and there's nothing we can do to stop them. But we can—and do—fight wildfires. This airplane is dropping fire retardant to slow the spread of a fire.

Smoke

The smoke from a wildfire can spread over a large area and affect people thousands of miles away. Fine particles of smoke can damage people's lungs. This smoke is especially dangerous for small children and people with breathing problems.

Firestorms

If a fire gets large enough, it creates its own weather. Hot, rising air sucks wind into the center of the fire. It rises high into the atmosphere, where it forms a storm cloud (called a pyrocumulus). This cloud may generate lightning that strikes many miles away, starting new fires.

Fire tornado

Rarely, the updraft from a fire begins to rotate and creates a fiery tornado. Smaller versions of these spinning columns of fire are called fire whirls.

Pandemic • **The biggest killer**

When a serious infectious disease spreads to many countries—or the whole world—in a short period of time, it's called a pandemic. Throughout history, pandemics have killed more people, by far, than any other natural disaster. These diseases are caused by viruses or bacteria, organisms too small to see without a microscope.

Small and smaller

As tiny as bacteria are, viruses are even smaller. They are not alive, but not exactly dead. A virus doesn't do anything until it gets into the cell of a living organism. Then it reproduces by turning the cell into a factory to make thousands of copies of itself, which go on to infect more cells.

Three pandemics

Historians believe that these were three of the deadliest pandemics of the past two thousand years. The pie charts show the estimated percentage (in red) of the world's population that perished in each pandemic.

About 70 million bubonic plague bacteria could fit in a circle this size.

But 80 billion influenza viruses could fit in the same circle.

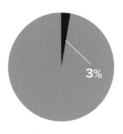

Justinian Plague
541–542
world population: 200 million
deaths: 50 million
25%

Black Death
1347–1351
world population: 400 million
deaths: 200 million
50%

influenza pandemic
1918
world population: 1,800 million
deaths: 50 million
3%

An influenza virus (left) and a bubonic plague bacterium (right) (both enlarged 15,000 times)

Black Death: the worst of them all

Bubonic plague is also known as the Black Death. Bubonic plague pandemics have probably killed more people than any other. There are still a few small outbreaks of the plague today. Fortunately, we can now cure this disease.

Bubonic plague bacteria were transmitted to humans by flea bites. Rats carried the fleas from place to place.

Spread of the plague, 1347–1351

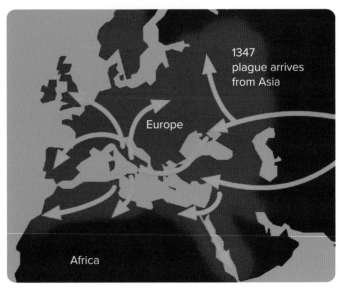

1347 plague arrives from Asia

Europe

Africa

There have been many outbreaks of the plague over the centuries. The worst was in the fourteenth century, when as much as half the world's population died. As many as 200 million people may have perished in this pandemic.

A success story

Smallpox rivals the plague as the deadliest disease in human history. Millions around the world died as repeated smallpox pandemics erupted.

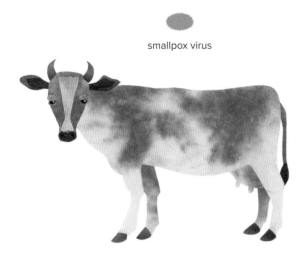

smallpox virus

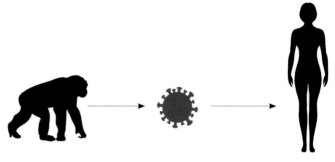

HIV AIDS virus

Smallpox was caused by a virus. Cowpox is a similar but much less deadly disease. In 1796, an English doctor took pus from the sores of a woman with cowpox and inserted it into the arm of a young boy. The child was protected against smallpox—it was the first successful vaccination. In 1980, smallpox was officially declared eradicated. This is considered the world's greatest public health achievement.

A modern plague

In the 1980s, HIV AIDS, a disease that had jumped from chimpanzees to people, was recognized by science. Since then, 32 million people around the world have died from AIDS, which damages the body's immune system. AIDS can be controlled with medicine, but hundreds of thousands of people, mostly in underdeveloped countries, die of the disease every year.

A flu pandemic

In 1918, an especially virulent strain of influenza—the flu—spread around the globe. It was the worst pandemic in recent history, killing more than 50 million people.

A new threat

In China in late 2019, a virus thought to have moved from bats to humans began to make people sick. The virus was similar to others that cause flu, but it was more contagious and more lethal. It causes a disease know as COVID-19. Millions of people around the world have died from the virus.

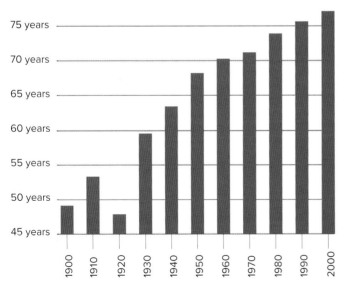

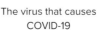

The virus that causes COVID-19

This graph shows the increase in average life expectancy in the United States from 1900 to 2000. There's a big decline just after 1918 due to deaths from the flu pandemic.

The virus is spread through tiny droplets coughed, sneezed, or breathed out. Wearing a mask is one of the best ways to protect against spreading or contracting the disease.

FUTURE OF THE EARTH

T he Earth is constantly changing—and has been for billions of years. It's been quite the evolution to get to where we are today . . . from gas, dust, and rocks, to being covered in water and then ice, and eventually forming continents and oceans and giving life to billions of humans, plants, and animals. So how does our planet continue to change? Where are we headed? And what's in store for the future of the Earth?

In this chapter, we'll look at some possible threats that are both distant in time and space, as well as the impact that humans have had over time and continue to have today. What does climate change mean for the future of the Earth as we know it? And what can we do to help protect and care for our planet today?

* Words in blue can be found in the glossary on page 154.

Protecting the planet

There is not much chance of a large asteroid or comet striking Earth anytime soon. But when it comes to world-changing impacts, it's a matter of *when,* not *if.* Sooner or later—it could be next week or thousands of years from now—a dangerous object will be headed right for us.

A recent event

In 2013, a meteor about 66 feet (20 meters) wide streaked through the sky above Chelyabinsk, a city in Russia. It disintegrated in the air and exploded with the force of a nuclear bomb. The blast damaged thousands of buildings and injured more than 1,500 people, most by flying glass. Luckily, no one was killed.

An asteroid (or piece of an asteroid or comet) that burns up in Earth's atmosphere is called a *meteor.* If it hits the ground, it is called a *meteorite.*

—— Estimated size of the 2013 Russian meteor

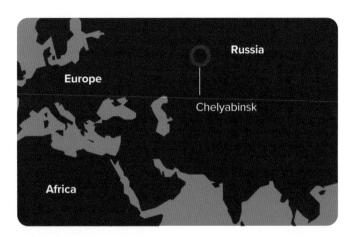

What can we do?

If we find an asteroid that is likely to hit our planet, we will need to change its orbit so that it misses us. Here are a few of the ways we might prevent a collision.

Ram it

One idea is to crash a satellite into the asteroid. If we find the object early enough, we'll only have to nudge it slightly. This will move it into a new orbit that misses us.

Zap it

Another concept involves firing lasers at the asteroid. The lasers will vaporize some of the rocky surface, creating a force that shoves the object into a different orbit.

Tug it

If we have enough time, parking a heavy spaceship next to the asteroid might work. The gravity of the ship will slowly tug the object onto a different path.

Nuke it

Unlike in the movies, we wouldn't want to blow up the asteroid. This could result in a lot of smaller pieces still headed toward Earth. But a nuclear bomb set off at a greater distance from the asteroid might push it out of a collision course.

Distant danger

Astronomers have witnessed events far from Earth—some of them incredibly violent—that could be disastrous for life on our planet if they were closer. Fortunately, most of them are so distant and infrequent that they are unlikely to affect us for millions or billions of years.

A rogue planet

A rogue planet is one that once orbited a star, but was ejected from its solar system. Perhaps another star passed close by and its gravity kicked the planet out of its orbit. There may be billions of these dark, solitary planets drifting through space. Could one collide with Earth? Luckily, space is so big and empty that there is very little chance of this happening.

Supernova

An aging large star can collapse and explode, briefly outshining its entire galaxy. This explosion is called a supernova. One occurring closer than 30 light years would bombard our planet with enough energy to cause mass extinctions. A supernova occurs this close to us only about once every 240 million years. Astronomers believe that we are safe for now.

Gamma ray burst

A gamma ray burst, or GRB, is a rare and violent release of energy when a large star implodes. These distant events are more powerful than anything we've seen in the universe. If a GRB happens within a few thousand light years of us, the radiation could destroy much of Earth's protective ozone layer and allow harmful radiation from the Sun to reach the surface.

The ultimate disaster

Like all stars, our Sun will die. In about five billion years, it will become a red giant. It will grow so large that it may engulf and vaporize Earth. Long before that happens, the Sun will grow hot enough to boil away the oceans and end life on our planet. But don't worry—that won't happen for another billion years or so.

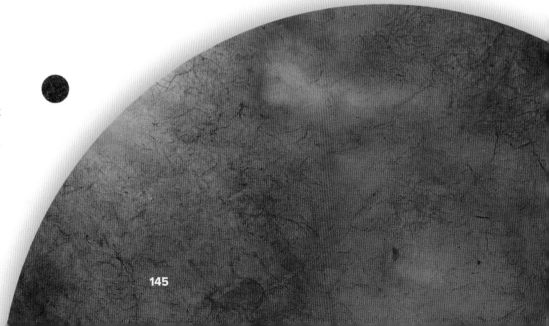

Climate change

Over millions of years, Earth's temperature has varied. At times, the planet was covered in ice and snow. Other periods have seen higher temperatures—even forests at the South Pole. Now the planet is getting warmer. And it's heating up much more quickly than in the past. Humans are responsible for most of this change. For the past 150 years, we've been burning fossil fuels that add greenhouse gases to the atmosphere.

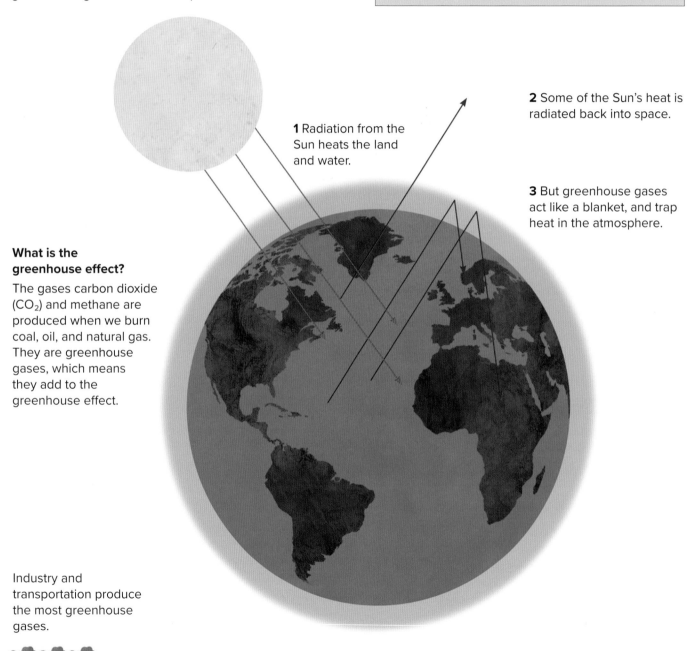

What's the difference between weather and climate?
Weather describes conditions in the atmosphere over a short period of time: How hot, cold, wet, dry, or windy is it? Weather changes from day to day and is different in different places. Climate also changes and varies with location. But climate describes these changes over a period of years, decades, or centuries.

1 Radiation from the Sun heats the land and water.

2 Some of the Sun's heat is radiated back into space.

3 But greenhouse gases act like a blanket, and trap heat in the atmosphere.

What is the greenhouse effect?

The gases carbon dioxide (CO_2) and methane are produced when we burn coal, oil, and natural gas. They are greenhouse gases, which means they add to the greenhouse effect.

Industry and transportation produce the most greenhouse gases.

Agriculture and deforestation also add greenhouse gases to the atmosphere. This is because cows belch a surprising amount of methane, and living trees absorb and store carbon dioxide.

Global temperature change and atmospheric carbon dioxide

Carbon dioxide in the atmosphere is measured in parts per million (ppm). This graph show how Earth's temperature has risen over the past 140 years as CO_2 concentrations have increased.

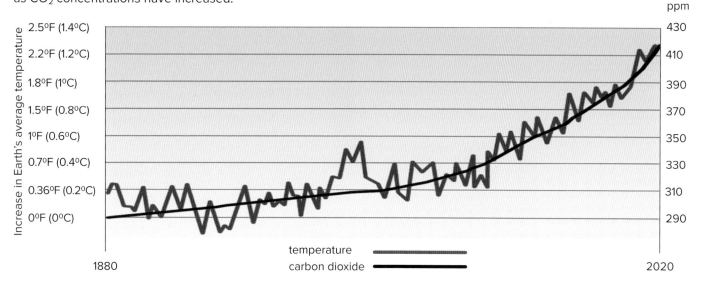

Changes caused by global warming are already showing up.

Changing seasons

In many parts of the world, spring is coming earlier and fall is arriving later.

Melting ice caps

The polar regions are losing ice at a rapid rate. Animals that depend on the ice floes for hunting and safety are becoming endangered.

Spreading tropical diseases

Ticks, mosquitoes, and other organisms that live in warm climates and spread disease are moving into parts of the world that used to be too cold for them.

Vanishing glaciers

All over the world, glaciers are melting or moving faster.

More powerful storms

Warmer ocean water produces stronger hurricanes.

More intense fires

Wildfires are burning hotter and longer as rising temperatures dry out vegetation.

It's getting hotter

We're just beginning to see the effects of a hotter climate. These effects will become more apparent—and more serious—as time goes on.

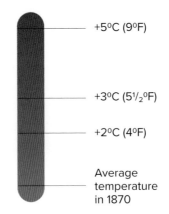

+5°C (9°F)

+3°C (5½°F)

+2°C (4°F)

Average temperature in 1870

How hot will it get?

Our goal is to limit warming to less than 2°C (4°F) above pre-industrial levels by 2100. Many scientists believe a 3°C (5½°F) figure is more likely. And if we continue to burn increasing amounts of fossil fuels, a 5°C (9°F) increase is possible. (*Scientists use degrees Celsius (°C) when referencing global warming, so those units appear first on these pages.*)

The climate change feedback loop

Many of the effects of climate change have a feedback effect, which causes a warming planet to heat up even faster.

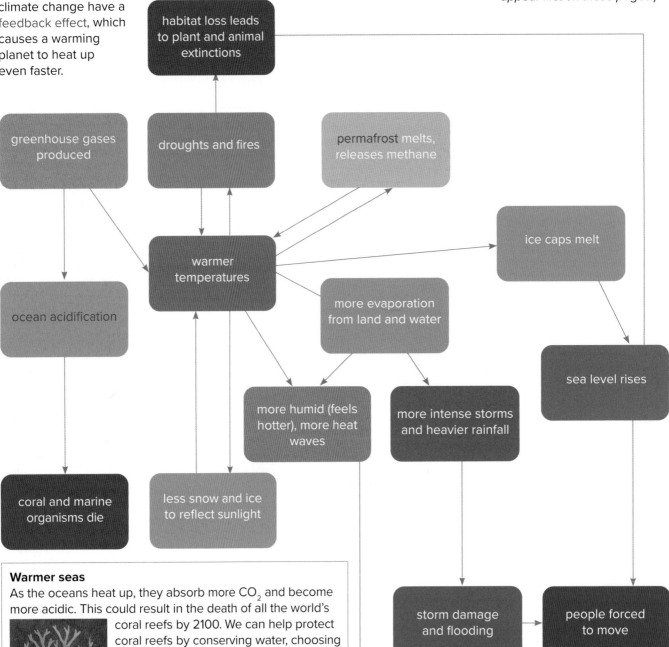

- habitat loss leads to plant and animal extinctions
- greenhouse gases produced
- droughts and fires
- permafrost melts, releases methane
- warmer temperatures
- ice caps melt
- ocean acidification
- more evaporation from land and water
- sea level rises
- more humid (feels hotter), more heat waves
- more intense storms and heavier rainfall
- coral and marine organisms die
- less snow and ice to reflect sunlight
- storm damage and flooding
- people forced to move

Warmer seas

As the oceans heat up, they absorb more CO_2 and become more acidic. This could result in the death of all the world's coral reefs by 2100. We can help protect coral reefs by conserving water, choosing sustainable seafood, and not sending chemicals into our waterways through certain sunscreens and fertilizers.

Ice caps

Most of the world's fresh water exists in the form of ice and snow. And 99 percent of that frozen water is held in the ice caps of Greenland and Antarctica. This ice is melting at a rapidly increasing rate. Still, it will take thousands of years for it to disappear completely.

Greenland and Antarctica shown at true relative size

Sea level rise

Since 1880, sea level has risen by more than eight inches.

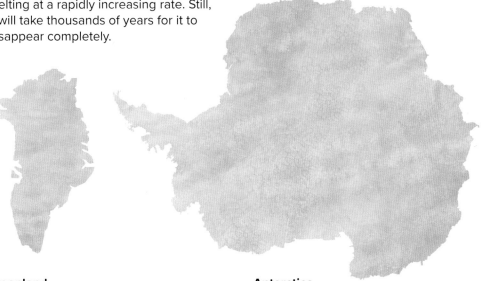

Greenland

About 9 percent of the world's ice is in Greenland, where the ice cap is 14,000 feet (4,267 meters) deep in some places. If all this ice were to melt, it would raise sea level by 25 feet (8 meters).

Antarctica

The continent at the South Pole holds 90 percent of the world's ice. The oceans would rise about 200 feet (61 meters) if all this ice melted.

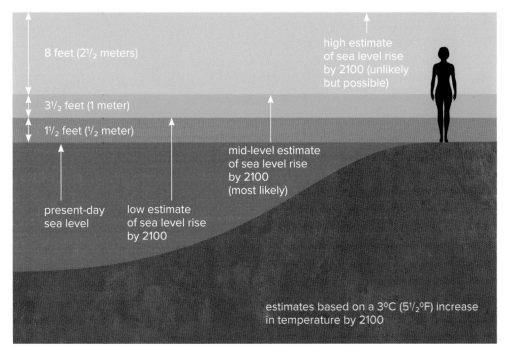

8 feet (2¹/₂ meters)

3¹/₂ feet (1 meter)

1¹/₂ feet (¹/₂ meter)

high estimate of sea level rise by 2100 (unlikely but possible)

mid-level estimate of sea level rise by 2100 (most likely)

present-day sea level

low estimate of sea level rise by 2100

estimates based on a 3°C (5¹/₂°F) increase in temperature by 2100

Actual sea level rise over the past 140 years (8¹/₂ inches • 22 centimeters)

sea level in 2020

2000

1980

1960

1940

1920

1900

sea level in 1880

The water is rising

One of the most visible effects of a warmer climate is sea level rise. Some of this rise is a result of ocean water expanding as it gets warmer. As time goes on, however, much of it will be from melting ice caps. A 3¹/₂ foot (1 meter) rise in sea level would flood many coastal cities around the world and displace millions of people.

Our climate impact

Climate prediction is complex, and we could experience dramatic, unexpected changes. Much will depend upon how successful the world can be at reducing greenhouse gas emissions. There are plenty of things humans can do, both small and large, to help the environment and combat the most serious effects of climate change.

Greenhouse gas emissions per country

Factors like population growth, economic development, energy use, land use, deforestation, agriculture, technology, and policies affect global greenhouse gas emissions. Knowing each country's emissions will allow them to work together by sharing best practices and strategies for reducing emissions.

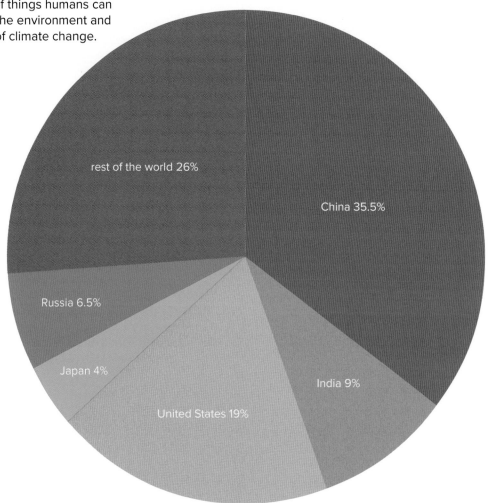

Do we have time to prevent the most serious effects of climate change?

With the current energy policies of governments, the world's CO_2 emissions are projected to decrease slightly by 2050. To keep global warming to only 1.5°C above pre-industrial temperatures, we will need to decrease emissions more rapidly while actively removing greenhouse gases from the atmosphere, reaching net-zero emissions by 2050.

current policy

net zero 2050 (<2°C)

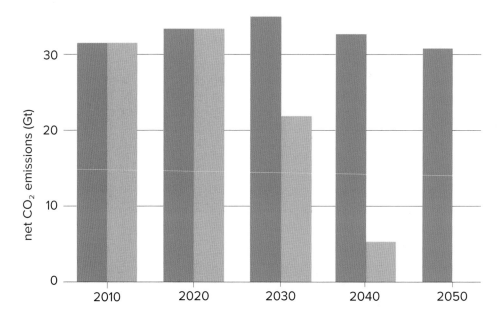

Plastic can take 1,000 years to degrade. But instead of breaking down over time, it breaks up into microplastics that are harmful to wildlife and the environment. Replacing single-use plastics like water bottles, straws, and plastic bags with reusable alternatives is an important first step in reducing plastic waste.

Carbon footprint of some of our choices

5 kg CO$_2$e

50 kg CO$_2$e

*tofu (20 g protein)
0.4 kg CO$_2$e

⟨

electric vehicle (driving for one hour at 45 mph)
5.9 kg CO$_2$e

new T-shirt
7 kg CO$_2$e

*beef (20 g protein, about a hamburger)
10 kg CO$_2$e

gas vehicle (driving for one hour at 45 mph)
18 kg CO$_2$e

flight from NYC to London (one passenger)
880 kg CO$_2$e

Landfills produce 20X more carbon dioxide emissions than composting

When food scraps are thrown in the trash, they end up in a landfill, producing 20X more carbon dioxide emissions (CO$_2$e) than when composted.

Composting can reduce household waste by 30 percent, and also helps reduce soil fertilization costs and increases the volume of water in soil so less frequent watering is needed.

It is estimated that one-third of our food is lost or wasted. Minimizing loss and waste would save the agricultural land and water use. This would cut down on nitrogen pollution and all the other emissions that are created when producing and transporting the food.

* world average emissions

Changing how we get and use energy

Slowing global warming will require a transition in the sources we use for energy (and how much we use). We will need to decrease the use of fossil fuels and increase renewable energy while transitioning to electric technologies for transport and heating. With investments in technologies like flexible power grids, electric car charging, energy storage, interconnected hydropower, and green hydrogen, the makeup of the world's energy sources could look like this in 2050 if we are on track to keep warming to less than 2°C this century.

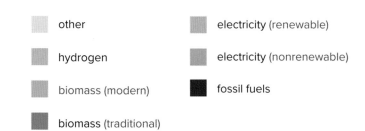

- other
- hydrogen
- biomass (modern)
- biomass (traditional)
- electricity (renewable)
- electricity (nonrenewable)
- fossil fuels

Total energy consumption

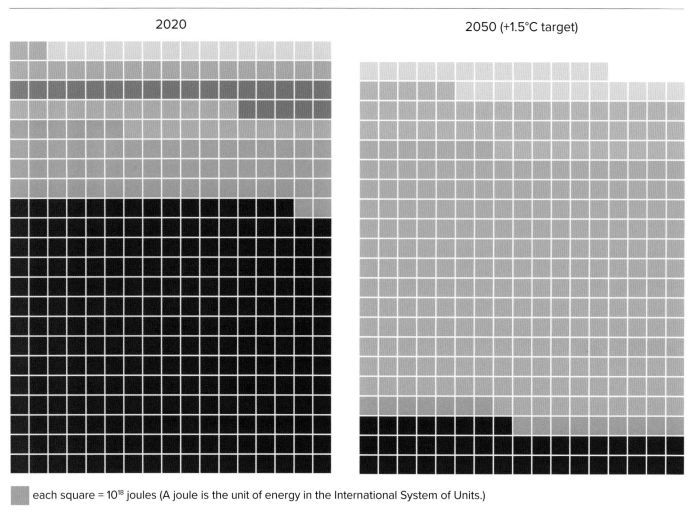

2020

2050 (+1.5°C target)

each square = 10^{18} joules (A joule is the unit of energy in the International System of Units.)

Geoengineering

Some scientists are proposing engineering solutions to the problem of climate change. These include spraying reflective substances from jets flying high in the atmosphere or finding ways to capture CO_2 and store it underground.

Renewable energy is getting cheaper

As technology improves and industries develop, solar and wind power costs are falling. Utility-scale solar panels and onshore wind farms are now competitive with power plants that burn fossil fuels to produce electricity.

Energy produced with $1*

= 2 kWh

One kilowatt-hour (kWh) is the amount of energy required to run a 1000-watt appliance, such as a microwave or coffee maker, for one hour.

Solar	Wind (onshore)		Gas†	Solar	Wind (onshore)
2010				2021	

\$1 in USD 2021, levelized, unsubsidized cost
† US gas combined cycle plant

Using energy and land more efficiently

In 2015, the world average amount of agricultural land used per person was down to 43 percent of the amount used per person in 1950.

In developed economies (OECD countries),* the energy used per person in 2022 was 88 percent of the energy used per person in 2004.

These trends will need to continue into the future if we hope to keep global warming to less than 2°C in this century and minimize the loss of wildlife habitats.

* Organization for Economic Cooperation and Development

The amount of electricity generated by solar and wind energy is growing quickly

In 2023 in the US, around 54 percent of the new ultility-scale electric capacity came from solar power and 11 percent came from wind.

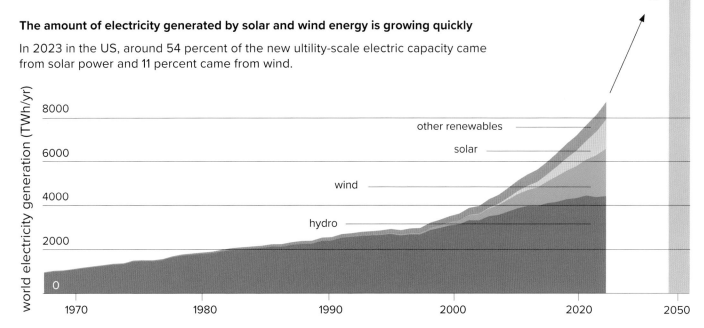

projected generation from all renewable sources = 38,000 TWh/yr

TWh: terawatt-hour is a unit of energy that is equal to 10^{12} watt-hours

abyssal zone
The deep, dark depths of the sea. This zone lies between 13,000 feet (3,962 meters) and 20,000 feet (6,096 meters) below the ocean's surface.

ancient
A time long ago; in the distant past.

anvil
A heavy metal block with a flat surface used for pounding other pieces of metal—which are often heated—into specific shapes (such as a horseshoe).

armored
Covered with protective plates or scales.

asteroid
A rocky, irregularly shaped object that circles the Sun.

Asteroids range from a few feet to 600 miles (966 kilometers) across.

astronomer
A scientist who studies space and the objects in it, including planets, moons, stars, and comets.

atmosphere
The gases—held in place by gravity—around a star, planet, or moon.

bacteria
Tiny, one-celled organisms. They are too small to see without magnification.

biomass
The total weight of the plants and/or animals in a specific area.

bombarded
Struck repeatedly with objects.

breached
Broken or ruptured. In the case of a dike, a breach is an opening made so that the water being held back can escape.

carbon dioxide
A colorless gas that exists naturally in Earth's atmosphere. It is used by plants to make food and exhaled in the breath of animals.

climate change
The gradual increase in global temperatures, changes in patterns of precipitation, and sea level rise. These changes are mostly caused by humans burning coal, oil, and other fossil fuels.

Copernicus
A Polish astronomer who lived about 500 years ago. He realized that rather than being at the center of the universe, Earth orbits the Sun.

continent
A large body of land. The Earth is usually considered to have seven continents.

debris
Loose or broken pieces of rock or other material.

deforestation
Cutting down or burning trees over a large area.

depleted
Decreased supply; used up.

devastating
Disastrous; especially destructive.

diameter
The distance across something; twice the radius.

diamonds
The element carbon in the form of a crystal. Diamonds are one of the hardest substances we know of. They are used as gemstones and can be extremely valuable.

dikes
Built-up soil, sand, or other material used to hold back the waters of a river, lake, or sea.

disorientation
Confusion, loss of a sense of direction or purpose.

drought
A long period of time with less rain- or snowfall than normal.

dwarf planet
An object that orbits the Sun. It is large enough for its own gravity to pull it into a round shape, but it is not a planet.

energy equivalent
A way to measure the amount of energy in one fuel source by comparing it to the amount of energy in another fuel source.

environment
Everything—including soil, water, temperature, vegetation, and animals—that surrounds a place or living thing.

equator
An imaginary line halfway between the North and South Poles that divides the Earth into equal hemispheres.

eradicate
To completely get rid of something. Eradication can be local (killing all the cockroaches in a building) or global (as in the worldwide elimination of the smallpox virus).

evolved
Changes in an animal's form or abilities that developed over many generations in response to changes in habitat, climate, or interactions with other animals.

extinct
No longer living. The term is applied to a particular species or group of organisms, not an individual.

Galileo
An Italian astronomer and scientist who lived about 400 years ago. He built one of the first telescopes and used it to observe the solar system.

gas
Matter that has no fixed shape or volume. A gas will fill whatever container holds it.

feedback effect
When the output of a system or process is fed back into the same process. The feedback effect can magnify the consequences of a process.

flare
A sudden burst of brightness on the Sun's surface.

fossil fuels
Gas, coal, and oil—fuels created by the remains of plants and animals that lived millions of years ago.

glacier
A large mass of ice formed by snow building up over many years. If the ground is sloped, the glacier will slowly move downhill.

gravity
The force that attracts matter to other matter. It holds moons and planets together and keeps them in an orbit around the Sun.

groundwater
Water found in the spaces between underground particles of soil and rock.

habitat loss
The destruction of the places animals live. Habitats can be lost due to natural causes, such as a hurricane or wildfire. Often it's due to human activity such as clearing forests for farms or cities.

human ancestors
Relatives of modern humans that lived between two million and 200,000 years ago.

humidity
A measure of the amount of water vapor in the air. Warm air holds more moisture than cold air. Humidity is measured as a percentage of the amount of water vapor that can exist in the air at a given temperature. One hundred percent humidity means that the air can contain no more moisture.

hydroelectric power
Electricity generated by falling or flowing water.

iceberg
A large, floating chunk of ice that breaks off of a glacier.

ice cap
A thick layer of ice that covers a large area or entire continent.

ice sheet
A layer of ice that covers a large area, but not as large as an ice cap. It can be on land or floating on water.

immune system
A network of cells and systems in the body that fight disease-causing organisms.

implode
To collapse violently. A large star implodes to become a black hole.

Indricotherium
An extinct relative of the modern rhinoceros. It lived about 20 million years ago in Asia, and was the largest mammal to ever live on land. It stood 18 feet (5½ meters) tall and weighed as much as five African elephants.

infographics
Facts and information presented visually as diagrams, charts, and graphs rather than just text.

invertebrates
Animals without a backbone, including insects, worms, jellyfish, and many other creatures.

kilometer
The kilometer is a metric unit of distance equal to $^6/_{10}$ of a mile.

landmass
A continent or large body of land.

lava flows
Rivers or sheets of red-hot, melted rock that flow from a volcano or from a volcanic vent.

light year
The distance light travels in one year. Light moves at 186,000 miles per second (300,000 kilometers per second). In a year, light will travel almost six trillion miles ($9^1/_2$ trillion kilometers).

lunar
Relating to the Moon.

mantle
A layer of the Earth that lies between the crust and the core. Due to the heat of the Earth's interior, it is partially molten.

mass extinction
An event that kills at least half of all living plant and animal species. There have been at least five mass extinctions over the past 450 million years.

matter
A substance that has mass and takes up space.

median
The midpoint in an ordered series of numbers.

meteorite
A meteor is a small, rocky object from space. Meteors burn up in the Earth's atmosphere. A meteorite is a meteor that doesn't completely burn up and hits the surface.

methane
A colorless, flammable gas that is produced by the breakdown of vegetation. Methane is the main component of the natural gas we often use to heat our homes.

microbes, or microscopic organisms
Forms of life that are too small to see without magnification, including bacteria, viruses, and fungi.

Milky Way Galaxy
The galaxy that contains our Sun and hundreds of billions of other stars.

molten
Melted.

nausea
An uneasy feeling in the stomach that may lead to throwing up.

Northern Hemisphere
The part of the globe north of the equator.

nuclear energy
Energy produced by splitting uranium atoms in a process called fission. Heat from this reaction is used to generate electricity.

ocean acidification
Carbon dioxide gas in the atmosphere dissolves in ocean water and makes carbonic acid, which is harmful to living things in the sea.

orbit
The path of one body in space around another, such as Earth's path around the Sun.

organisms
Any living thing, including plants, animals, and single-cell life forms.

partial
Part of something; not complete.

particles
Tiny pieces of matter.

permafrost
Soil found in the polar regions and at high altitudes that remains frozen year-round. Large areas of permafrost are thawing as the climate warms, with potentially serious consequences that we don't fully understand.

perpetual
Constant, continuous.

phenomenon
An observed event that is often unusual or impressive.

poaching
Illegal hunting. Animals may be shot, trapped, or poisoned for food, trophies, or body parts that are sold illegally.

precipitation
Rain, snow, hail, or sleet; water in any form that falls to the ground as part of a natural process.

predators
Animals that kill and eat other animals.

pre-industrial
A time before the industrial revolution (which began in the late 1700s) and before the widespread use of heavy machinery and fossil fuels.

prey
An animal that is hunted and eaten by other animals.

radioactive elements
Matter composed of unstable atoms that emit particles and release energy.

red giant
A giant star with a cooler surface that glows red. It is one of the last stages of a star's life.

reptile
A group of egg-laying animals with scaly skin, including turtles, lizards, snakes, and crocodiles.

retardant
A substance that slows or stops an event or process, such as a fire.

rotation
Spinning or rotating around an axis.

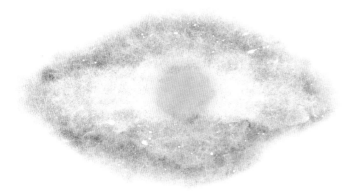

scientific instruments
Tools used to observe and measure natural or human-made events or processes.

scuba diving
Staying underwater for an extended time by using a self-contained breathing system and air storage tanks.

sea level rise
A gradual increase in the level of the ocean. It is caused by water expanding as it gets warmer and by the melting of glaciers and ice caps. We are experiencing sea level rise at an increasing rate.

Snowball Earth
A period about 650 million years ago when a thick layer of ice and snow covered the Earth from pole to pole. It lasted for millions of years. The ice melted when enough volcanoes erupted to change the atmosphere and heat the planet back up.

snowpack
A layer of accumulated snow that has not been compressed into ice.

solar power
Power generated by converting the sun's rays into electricity.

solar system
The gravitationally bound system of the Sun and the objects that orbit it. The largest of such objects are the eight planets.

species
A group of living things that look alike, behave in a similar way, and are able to produce offspring.

submersible
An underwater vessel often used for research. Unlike a submarine, it is connected to the surface or a supporting ship with cables that provide power and air.

sulfuric acid
A liquid chemical compound that can dissolve skin, metals, and many other substances.

trench
In the ocean, a long, narrow, and very deep valley in the seafloor. Trenches are the deepest spots in the ocean.

tsunami
A large wave or series of waves that are caused by a sudden change in the seafloor or ocean. Earthquakes, volcanoes, landslides, and meteorite impacts can all cause tsunamis.

turbulent
Jumbled and chaotic, moving rapidly in a disorderly way.

updraft
An upward movement of air. Hot air is lighter than cold air. In a fire, heated air rises, creating an updraft.

vaccination
The introduction, often by injection, of small amounts of a disease-causing virus or bacteria into a human or animal. These dangerous organisms are killed or made less virulent before being used in a vaccine. The vaccine causes the recipient's body to create antibodies to the disease—cells that will attack the dangerous form of the virus or bacteria if it is encountered.

vertebrate
An animal with a backbone. Fish, reptiles, amphibians, birds, and mammals are all vertebrates.

virulent
Extremely toxic or harmful.

vulnerable
Susceptible to harm or damage.

white dwarf
A very dense star that has used up most of its fuel and collapsed. When the Sun becomes a white dwarf, it will be about the size of Earth.

yellow dwarf
A star similar in size to the Sun that glows white or yellow. Our Sun is a yellow dwarf.

100 Most Destructive Natural Disasters. By Anna Claybourne. Scholastic, 2014.

Amazing Biofacts. By Susan Goodman. Peter Bedrick Books, 1993.

Amazing Animals Q&A. By David Burnie. DK Publishing, 2007.

Amazing Numbers in Biology. By Rainer Flindt. Springer, 1996.

The Animal Book. By Steve Jenkins. Houghton Mifflin Harcourt, 2013.

Animal Fact File. By Dr. Tony Hare. Checkmark Books, 1999.

Animal Records. By Mark Carwardine. Sterling, 2008.

Around the World: The Atlas for Today. Edited by Andrew Losowsky, Sven Ehmann, and Robert Klanten. Gestalten, 2013.

The Best Book of Volcanoes. By Simon Adams. Kingfisher, 2001.

Big Numbers. By Mary and John Gribbin. Wizard Books, 2003.

The Book of Comparisons. By Clive Gifford. Ivy Kids, 2018.

The Book of Life. Edited by Stephen J. Gould. W. W. Norton & Company, 1993

The Cambridge Photographic Guide to the Planets. By F. W. Taylor. Cambridge University Press, 2001.

The Complete Guide to Extreme Weather. By Louise Spilsbury and Anna Claybourne. Sandy Creek, 2016.

Cosmos: The Infographic Book of Space. By Stuart Lowe and Chris North. Aurum Press, 2015.

Digging for Bird Dinosaurs: An Expedition to Madagascar. By Nic Bishop. Houghton Mifflin, 2000.

Dinosaurs. Edited by Sherry Gerstein and Beverly Larsen. Reader's Digest Children's Books, 1999.

Dinosaurs: A Concise Natural History. By David E. Fastovsky and David B. Weishampel. Cambridge University Press, 2016.

Dinosaur Encyclopedia. Edited by Kitty Blount and Maggie Crowley. DK Publishing, 2001.

Dinosaurs: How They Lived and Evolved. By Darren Nash and Paul Barrett. Smithsonian Book, 2016.

DK Find Out! Solar System. DK Publishing, 2016.

Down, Down, Down. By Steve Jenkins. HMH Books for Young Readers, 2009.

The Dynamics of Disaster. By Susan W. Kieffer. W. W. Norton and Company, 2013.

The Earth Book. By Jonathan Litton. 360 Degrees, 2016.

Earth Explained. By Barbara Taylor. A Henry Holt Reference Book, 1997.

The Earth Pack: A Three-Dimensional Action Book. By Ron Van Der Meer. National Geographic Society, 1995.

Earth-Shattering Events. By Robin Jacobs. Cicada Books, 2020.

Egg: Nature's Perfect Package. By Steve Jenkins and Robin Page. Houghton Mifflin Harcourt, 2015.

Empire of the Sun. By John Gribben and Simon Goodwin. New York University Press, 1998.

The Encyclopedia of Animals. Edited by Dr. Per Christiansen. Amber Books, 2006.

Encyclopedia of Dinosaurs and Other Prehistoric Creatures. Edited by James Pickering. Backpack Books, 2002.

Everything Volcanoes and Earthquakes. By Kathy Furgang. National Geographic Children's Books, 2013.

Everything Weather. By Kathy Furgang. National Geographic Children's Books, 2012.

Fantastic Book of Comparisons. By Russell Ash. Dorling Kindersley, 1997.

Global Warming. By Seymour Simon. HarperCollins, 2013.

Incredible Earth. By Nick Clifford. DK Publishing, 1996.

The Infographic History of the World. By Valentina D'Efilippo and James Ball. Firefly Books, 2014.

Information Everywhere. Edited by Jenny Finch. DK Publishing, 2013.

Knowledge Is Beautiful. By David McCandless. Harper Design, 2014.

Life. By Martha Holmes and Michael Gunton. University of California Press, 2010.

The Life of Mammals. By David Attenborough. Princeton University Press, 2002.

Little Kids First Big Book of Dinosaurs. By Catherine D. Hughes. National Geographic Children's Books, 2011.

My Best Book of Volcanoes. By Simon Adams. Kingfisher, 2001.

National Geographic Animal Encyclopedia. By Jinny Johnson. Marshall Editions, 1999.

Natural Disasters. By Dougal Dixon. The Reader's Digest Association Limited, 1997.

Nature's Predators. By Michael Bright, Robin Kerrod, and Barbara Taylor. Hermes House, 2002.

Otherworlds: Visions of Our Solar System. By Michael Benson. Abrams, 2017.

Our Solar System. By Seymour Simon. Harper, 2014.

The Planets: The Definitive Visual Guide to Our Solar System. By Robert Dinwiddie. DK Publishing, 2014.

Prehistoric Predators. By Brian Switek. Applesauce Press, 2015.

Sciencia. By Burkard Polster, Matthew Watkins, Matt Tweed, Gerard Cheshire, and Moff Betts. Wooden Books, 2011.

The Sizesaurus. By Stephen Strauss. Kodansha International, 1995.

Sleep and Rest in Animals. By Corine Lacrampe. Firefly Books, 2003.

Solar System. By Marcus Chown. Black Dog & Leventhal, 2011.

Space Encyclopedia: A Tour of Our Solar System and Beyond. By David A. Aguilar. National Geographic Children's Books, 2013.

Supernavigators. By David Barrie. The Experiment, 2019.

Superstats: Extreme Planet. By Moira Butterfield. Little Bee Books, 2015.

Tornadoes! By Gail Gibbons. Holiday House, 2009.

The Ultimate Book of Dinosaurs. By Paul Dowswell, John Malam, Paul Mason, and Steve Parker. Paragon Publishing, 2003.

Venom, Poison, and Electricity. By Kimberley Jane Pryor. Marshall Cavendish, 2010.

Venom: Poisonous Animals in the Natural World. By Steve Backshall. New Holland Publishers, 2007.

Volcano & Earthquake. By Susanna Van Rose. DK Eyewitness Books, 2014

The Way Nature Works. Edited by Robin Rees. Macmillan, 1992.

Weird, Wild, Amazing! By Tim Flannery. Norton Young Readers, 2019.

Wildlife Factfinder. By Martin Walters. Dempsey Parr, 1999.

The World of Animals. By Desmond Morris. Jonathan Cape, 1993.

Animals, art, and books

The author and his research assistant

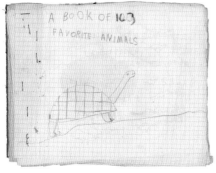

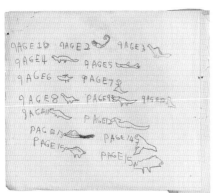

103 Animals, cover and table
of contents

When I was six years old, I was given a copy of *Life* magazine. On the cover was a remarkable illustration of a bird and a tortoise. Inside, I found an article describing Charles Darwin's 1835 voyage to the Galápagos Islands. The illustrations of marine iguanas, giant tortoises, and blue-footed boobies were fascinating. I cut out the pictures, pasted them into a blank journal, and wrote my own captions. The journal is long gone, but I remember it clearly, down to the way the pictures buckled a little from the paste I used to glue them down.

My interest in books and animals didn't begin with that magazine. I had, in fact, already written and illustrated a volume titled *103 Animals*. At the time, I imagined these stapled-together sheets of graph paper to be an in-depth survey of the animal kingdom. My credibility as a nature writer was enhanced by the small menagerie of insects, turtles, lizards, and other local wildlife that shared my bedroom.

When I grew up, I became an illustrator and graphic designer. I founded a business and started a family. Still, I never lost my interest in nature and science. And thirty-five years after I came across that *Life* magazine, my first book was published. Since then I've illustrated and written—or cowritten with Robin Page, my wife and creative partner—more than thirty books about the natural world.

—Steve Jenkins

More books by Steve Jenkins or Steve Jenkins and Robin Page:

Actual Size.
Houghton Mifflin Harcourt, 2004.

Almost Gone: The World's Rarest Animals.
HarperCollins, 2006.

Animals in Flight.
Written with Robin Page.
Houghton Mifflin Harcourt, 2001.

The Beetle Book.
Houghton Mifflin Harcourt, 2012.

Big and Little.
Houghton Mifflin Harcourt, 1996.

Biggest, Strongest, Fastest.
Houghton Mifflin Harcourt, 1995.

Bones.
Scholastic, 2010.

Dogs and Cats.
Houghton Mifflin Harcourt, 2007.

Down, Down, Down.
Houghton Mifflin Harcourt, 2009.

How Many Ways Can You Catch a Fly?
Written with Robin Page.
Houghton Mifflin Harcourt, 2008.

How to Clean a Hippopotamus.
Written with Robin Page.
Houghton Mifflin Harcourt, 2010.

I See a Kookaburra!
Written with Robin Page.
Houghton Mifflin Harcourt, 2005.

Just a Second.
Houghton Mifflin Harcourt, 2011.

Life on Earth: The Story of Evolution.
Houghton Mifflin Harcourt, 2002.

Living Color.
Houghton Mifflin Harcourt, 2007.

Move!
Written with Robin Page.
Houghton Mifflin Harcourt, 2006.

My First Day.
Written with Robin Page.
Houghton Mifflin Harcourt, 2013.

Never Smile at a Monkey.
Houghton Mifflin Harcourt, 2009.

Prehistoric Actual Size.
Houghton Mifflin Harcourt, 2005.

Sisters and Brothers.
Written with Robin Page.
Houghton Mifflin Harcourt, 2008.

Slap, Squeak, and Scatter.
Houghton Mifflin Harcourt, 2001.

Time for a Bath.
Written with Robin Page.
Houghton Mifflin Harcourt, 2011.

Time to Eat.
Written with Robin Page.
Houghton Mifflin Harcourt, 2011.

Time to Sleep.
Written with Robin Page.
Houghton Mifflin Harcourt, 2011.

What Do You Do When Something Wants to Eat You?
Houghton Mifflin Harcourt, 1997.

What Do You Do with a Tail Like This?
Written with Robin Page.
Houghton Mifflin Harcourt, 2003.

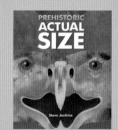
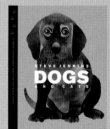
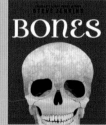

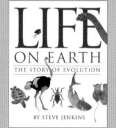

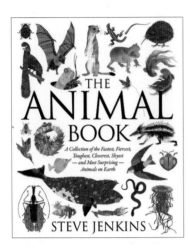
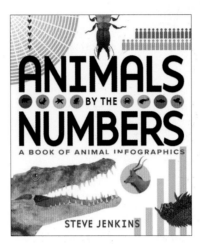
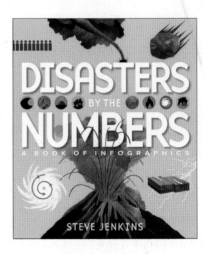

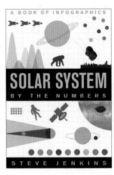

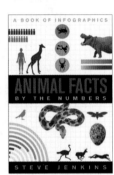

Clarion Books is an imprint of HarperCollins Publishers.

Library of Congress Control Number: 2023933194
ISBN 978-0-06-331571-6

The artist used torn- and cut-paper collage to create the illustrations for this book.

24 25 26 27 28 COS 10 9 8 7 6 5 4 3 2 1

First Edition